The Division Street
PRINCESS

The Division Street
PRINCESS

A MEMOIR

Elaine Soloway

SYREN BOOK COMPANY
MINNEAPOLIS

Most Syren Books are available at special quantity discounts for bulk purchases for sales promotions, premiums, fund-raising, and educational needs. For details, write

Syren Book Company
Special Sales Department
5120 Cedar Lake Road
Minneapolis, MN 55416

Published by
Syren Book Company
5120 Cedar Lake Road
Minneapolis, MN 55416

Printed in the United States of America on acid-free paper

ISBN-13: 978-0-929636-63-4
ISBN-10: 0-929636-63-5

LCCN 2006920905

Cover design by Kyle G. Hunter
Book design by Ann Sudmeier

Cover photo: Irv's Finer Foods in the early 1940s. Posing in front of our grocery store are my brother, Ronnie; my dad, Irving Shapiro; my mom, Min Elkin Shapiro; Dad's sister Mary; and me. The photographer was Mary's husband, Hy Cohen.

Photo editor: Renee Elkin

To order additional copies of this book, see the form at the back or go to www.itascabooks.com.

IN MEMORY OF MY PARENTS,

Min Elkin Shapiro and Irving Eugene Shapiro

I have changed the names and descriptions of various people to protect their privacy. Some characters are composites of people I have known. To make this story a more pleasurable read, I've compressed or changed the time line, imagined details, and invented dialogue.

He stood watching until after she'd gone inside, and until the tall windows of one room after another cast their sudden light into the darkness. Then more lights came on and more, room upon room, as Sally ventured deeper into the house she had always loved and probably always would—having it now, for the first time and at least for a little while, all to herself.

—*Richard Yates*
"Saying Goodbye to Sally"

Contents

The Division Street
PRINCESS

Daddy Wants a Bite of His American Dream

In 1942, the year I turned four, my father was a $17-a-week salesman at Blue Star Auto Supply on Milwaukee Avenue. And although he felt lucky to have a job since he never went to high school, let alone college, my father—Irving Eugene Shapiro—hungered for more: He wanted to be his own boss. So when he spotted the For Rent sign that was Scotch-taped to the plate glass window of the grocery store downstairs of our apartment, Dad took it as an omen that his fortunes would change.

It was an early evening in March of that year, and I was sitting in the kitchen of our three-room flat watching my mother cook dinner, when Dad burst through the door and proclaimed, "Let's buy the grocery store downstairs!" My 33-year-old father must have taken the steps two at time, for his face was flushed and he was starving for breath. His shirt and slacks—which were freshly ironed when he left at seven that morning—were now wrinkled and greasy, and his once clean-shaven face was whiskered and perspiring Valvoline motor oil instead of Old Spice.

I quickly turned my attention from the supper Mom

was stirring in the electric frying pan (ground beef browned in Wesson oil, macaroni, and Ragú spaghetti sauce) to Dad and his exuberant idea. The smells of Mom's "Chili Mac" momentarily muffled Dad, but he recovered and said, "It'll be perfect. Our very own business just one flight down. We can run it together—a mom-and-pop operation." Then, he approached his wife and, before attempting his usual homecoming kiss, took the red-coated spatula from her skinny fingers and brought the dripping spoon to his mouth. The look on my mother's face as she watched him seal his lips around the spoon was sadly familiar to me: It was one of irritation, disgust.

Even at that young age, I knew it wasn't only Dad's vulgar tasting that night that riled my mother, for the two of them sparred daily. "Stop eating, Irv, you'll kill yourself," was her most familiar jab, followed by his, "Leave me alone, if I can't eat, I'd rather die." Other bouts opened with, "We don't need it, we can't afford it, take it back, Irv." And his response, "Live a little, for God's sake." Whenever I heard their arguments, I'd duck for cover, like a recruit frightened of battle. And although the two of them never came to blows and seemed to recuperate quickly, my wounds took longer to heal.

"We'll make a space in the back of the store for the kids so you can keep an eye on them," Dad said to Mom as he returned her spoon to the pan. "I can see it now, Min and Irv's Finer Foods." He slid his palm across the air in front of him as if he were unfurling a banner with the store's name in neon. I followed his fingers, certain I could read the title, too. "We can be together all day," he said.

"I won't have to see you just in the evenings and week-ends. It'll be terrific!" That was the funny thing about my dad—although Mom opposed him on so many fronts, he was crazy in love with her and never wanted her out of his sight.

Who could blame him? At 29 years old, Min Elkin Shapiro was a beauty—the prettiest of the four Elkin girls, and as skinny as a pencil. She had blue eyes the color of Lake Michigan and wore her black hair piled on top of her hair in a pompadour style, like Dorothy Lamour. Unlike the wartime pinup, Mom was short, about 5'2", but because she always wore high-heeled shoes, appeared to be a bit taller than that. And Mom never left the house without her Max Factor Fire Engine Red lipstick, matching rouge, blue eye shadow, and coal black mascara. "You never know who you're going to meet," she'd say as I watched her paint her face before the grateful bathroom mirror.

"I don't know if it's such a good idea for you to be around food all day," Mom said to Dad, swapping an ash-tray for a saucer he was about to use.

He plucked a Camel from an open pack in his shirt pocket, lit it, and inhaled deeply. Then, resting the glowing cigarette on the ashtray's lip, he turned to me and said, "You'd like me around more, wouldn't you, Princess?" He scooped me up in his strong arms—a lift-up I loved be-cause I could feel Dad's biceps. When I would comment on the hard rocks stored on his upper arms, Dad would tell me how he got those muscles. "Swimming laps at the Divi-sion Street Y, the very same pool as Johnny Weissmuller." Although Dad may have had the strength of Tarzan of the

Jungle, he had the build of a wrestler. He was short—about 5'4"—with a broad chest, big belly, and his legs bore black-and-blue markings. Along with my nightly ride up to his chest, I also loved that my dad called me "Princess," for the pet name made me feel special, unlike the ordinary "Elaine" my mother used, or "peanut" from my older brother, Ronnie. "Princess"—dainty, pretty, protected—that's how I felt in my father's eyes, and in his brawny arms.

With my small arms around his neck, I brushed my fingers against his black hair—which he wore slicked back like the movie star George Raft—and kissed his rough cheek. "Yes, Daddy, yes," I said, meaning every word. "I'd love to have you around more."

Ronnie, almost seven years old, jumped up from his spot on the living room carpet, where he had been listening to *Captain Midnight* on our Emerson radio and asked, "Can I have a job in the store?"

"Of course," Dad said, unwrapping my arms from his neck and placing me back on my throne—a kitchen chair that held a Chicago Yellow Pages telephone book. "We'll all have jobs in the store."

"I don't know, Irv," Mom said, wiping her hands on a red-splotched apron that covered her Swirl housecoat. "What do we know about running a grocery store? And if you leave Blue Star, what'll we use for money until customers come?" Then, she turned to the cabinets above the sink, stood on tiptoes—even though she was wearing house slippers with a three-inch wedge—and pulled four dinner plates from the first shelf.

My parents' engagement picture. With her bobbed hair,
blue eyes, and lace dress, Mother looks like a socialite.
And Dad, in suit and tie, appears to be a substantial
young businessman.

"What's to know?" Dad said, patting his broad belly. "If there's anything I'm an expert on, it's food. Hell, I'm the best salesman they've got at Blue Star, and that's all it is—salesmanship. Instead of crankshafts and wheel rims, I'll be peddling salami and laundry soap—it's no different. And with your gorgeous *punim,* we'll have customers lining up around the block. Think about the store, that's all I ask," Dad said, and Mom agreed to do just that.

That evening, there was no further talk of the grocery as we all gathered in the living room to join Dad and Ronnie in one of their favorite activities: listening to the Friday night fights on the radio. Three years older than me, my brother was what you might call "jaunty." He had pretty eyes like my mom's—only his were brown like Dad's—black hair, and a big smile.

The fight on the evening of March 27 was more interesting for us because Joe Louis, the heavyweight champ of the world, was going to take on Abe Simon—a Jew! Our tribe had so few athletes to cheer for—you could count the baseball and football players on one hand, and maybe use two for wrestlers—that when one of our own entered the ring, it was a special occasion.

"I love Louis, don't get me wrong," Dad said, lowering himself into his armchair that was freckled with cigarette burns. "But Simon's six-four, 255 pounds, and Jewish. We gotta be in his corner."

On the table next to him, Dad placed a pack of Camels, an already filled ashtray, a large water pitcher filled to the top, and a bowl of Borden's chocolate ice cream. He had at first spooned three scoops of the dessert from its carton, but before it made its way to his side table, Mom had shaved off two of the scoops and plopped them into bowls for Ronnie and me. Dad kept silent when Mom monitored his food like that, because in the middle of the night, he would return to the freezer or pantry and enjoy his nosh alone. I knew this because I would sometimes bump into him on my way to the bathroom. Even if he forgot to put his finger to his lips to silence me, I'd never, ever, rat on my dad.

I also knew that Mom was worried about Dad's appetite because he was a diabetic and wasn't supposed to eat sugary foods. But I loved sweets, too, and couldn't understand how such wonderful-tasting stuff could be bad for you.

"Simon's got a shot," Ronnie said, inching himself closer to the Emerson. "He flattened Jersey Joe Wolcott in three rounds."

"Is Simon the guy that said 'I shall return'?" I asked from my corner of the sofa. I was already dressed in my flannel pajamas because I was likely to fall asleep on the spot and have to be hoisted to bed. Perched with my legs tucked under, I was about to attack one of my two favorite things from the table next to me: chocolate ice cream or a book—in this case, *Snow White and the Seven Dwarfs*. Although I was curious about the fight on the radio, I knew I'd be bored after a few rounds, and intended to turn to Snow White. I hadn't started school yet, but I loved books and carried them around with me wherever I went. I studied their pictures and tried to sound out the words, tracing

the letters one-by-one, as I had seen my brother do with
Dick and Jane.

"No, *shmegegge* [idiot], not Simon" Ronnie said to
me. "It was General MacArthur who said, 'I shall return'
when he pulled his troops from the Philippines."

Stung by his jab, I tried to explain that I was only able
to read the three big words in the *Daily News* headline,
and not the smaller type, but Dad stopped me and said,
"Shush, the fight's starting."

Mom took a seat on the sofa, pulled a ball of woolen
yarn from a canvas bag on the carpet, and began to work
on an afghan she had started earlier. As her needles rhyth-
mically clacked through the brown and white threads that
were wrapped around her fingers, I wondered if she was
concentrating on her knitting, or puzzling over Dad's
proposal. Please say yes, I urged in a telepathic message.
I sensed my father had his heart set on owning the store,
and I hated the thought of his being disappointed. Looking back, I must've believed—and perhaps Dad did, too—
that the grocery store was his big chance to prove himself
to Mom, to his kids, and to himself.

Not long after the announcer had introduced the fight-
ers, Dad said dully, "That's it." He rose from his chair, took
the emptied pitcher to the sink and refilled it. The referee
was proclaiming: one, two, three . . . over Simon's flattened
body. The 15-round fight at Madison Square Garden that
night ended at 6 when Louis knocked Simon's giant body
to the canvas for the full count. "So much for our big Jewish hero," Mom said, stabbing the needles back into the
ball of yarn.

"At least he gave it a shot," Dad said, and took a drink of water straight from the pitcher, as if he were the fighter in need of reviving.

That night, as I lay in the bed I shared with my brother, I could hear my parents' voices above the squeak of the Murphy bed they were lowering from the living room wall. As the mattress frame landed with a thud on the carpet, I tiptoed to the bedroom door and opened it just enough to eavesdrop. As I had hoped, they were discussing the store. "If it'll make you feel better, I'll ask Maury, Jack, and Pa to check it out," Dad said. "The three wise men—a butcher, fruit peddler, and fishmonger." I heard Dad chuckle, and hoped that Mom was smiling at his joke, too.

That's a good idea, I thought. Call in her brothers-in-law and her father. I quietly closed the door and padded back to bed. I knew it was silly to ask Dad's own brothers for business advice, for he had once told me of their earlier joint venture. It happened before I was born, and when Dad related the story of three of the four Shapiro boys' money-losing barbecue stand, I had pictured Dad, Ben, and Jim as the Three Stooges—Curly, Moe, and Larry—colliding into each other while pounds of spareribs blackened in a pit. No, Mom's side of the family was definitely the way to go.

So that's how one balmy Sunday in April, 1942, two uncles on my mother's side and her father accompanied my family as we toured the vacant space at 2505 W. Division St., in Chicago's Humboldt Park neighborhood, that was to become the centerpiece of my childhood.

Maurice Kaplan, who was married to Mom's younger sister Etta, was the butcher among the three wise men. An immigrant from Poland, Uncle Maury was also the family scholar. He read the *Jewish Daily Forward* in Yiddish, spoke several additional languages, and walked 10 miles a day for exercise and contemplation.

"Where would you put the meat, Maury?" my dad asked, his hand reaching up to clasp his brother-in-law's shoulder. Although I didn't know it at the time, my uncle, who still had family in Poland, was more worried about their survival that day than my family's fortunes. For on March 28, British and U.S. Intelligence learned of the Nazis' plans "to eradicate all of Europe's Jews." My uncle revealed none of his anguish, and instead told my dad, "Meat should be in the back, near the walk-in freezer." He pointed his rolled-up newspaper in that direction, and I pictured slabs of beef hanging from hooks in the frigid locker. I shook away the image and studied my uncle. With his dark hair already graying at the temples, and dressed in a spotless white button-down shirt and brown slacks, Uncle Maury looked distinguished, more like a professor than a storefront butcher.

Our landlady, Mrs. Newman, a dark-haired woman in her 40s, was also on the tour that day. Although she collected rent on the 12 apartments in our fading brown brick building, as well as all the ground-floor shops—and who knows how many other properties—Mrs. Newman dressed like a bag lady. Perhaps to trick any *schnorrers* (beggars) who might approach, she wore secondhand clothes two sizes too large, men's shoes, and she carried a balding leather pocketbook stuffed with legal-looking papers, receipt books, and mail.

"I'll give you a good deal," Mrs. Newman said to my parents, as she rummaged through the debris in her purse. "Business will boom before you know it."

And if on that mild April day, you were to look out the store's front door that was propped open for fresh air, you might have echoed her optimism. Even with the boys overseas—including my mother's four brothers—Division Street bustled with people, immigrants with big families like my parents'.

And those that remained on the home front—like my father, who was 4-F, or housewives rationing provisions, or women taking over shifts in factories and offices—all seemed to be energized with patriotic zeal. I remember the day the government announced its "Salvage for Victory" campaign and neighbors rallied together in the empty lot next to our building to donate tin, rubber, scrap iron, rags, and paper for the war effort. I suppose Dad must have been encouraged by that camaraderie and believed these same neighbors would eagerly crowd into our grocery store and help him satisfy his American dream.

"Just picture it, honey," Dad said, focusing a sales pitch on my mother. "We'll hang kosher salami and bologna from strings above the deli counter."

I closed my eyes and as he described the foods that would fill the store, I sniffed the fragrances that could spill from garlicky pickles and fat corned beef. And I could almost taste the sweet halvah, the crusty ryes, the buttery strudels. My stomach rumbled as I watched for Mom's reaction, but her blue eyes were wide open as she asked Mrs. Newman, "What's the monthly rent?"

"Later, Min, later," the landlady said, grabbing Mom's elbow and guiding her towards the bare ice cream cooler. "First, look around. Look at the fixtures they left."

My dad turned from the two women, ground out a cigarette stub with his shoe, lit another Camel, and said to my uncle Jack, the fruit peddler in the family, "What about fruits and vegetables?" Jack Silver, who was married to Mom's older sister Mollie, was dressed in an unbuttoned short-sleeved shirt that revealed his ribbed undershirt. This brother-in-law sold goods that he selected at dawn from sprawling produce markets on the West Side. Uncle Jack piled his potatoes, onions, watermelon, and more in a truck he inched up and down Chicago alleys.

Housewives would perch on their rickety wooden back steps and shout their orders to the wiry *shtarker* (strong guy) down below.

"In the front, Irv," Uncle Jack said. "The bananas and tomatoes should hit them the minute they step foot in the door."

Mrs. Newman followed close behind my parents as they inspected the empty display cases and traced their fingers across dusty shelves.

"Before you know it, Irv, the war will be over and all those GIs will be marching back, filling Division Street with *kinderlach,* filling your register with *gelt,*" she said, shaking a lease she had unearthed from her purse.

"What do you think?" Dad asked my *zadie,* owner

of Elkin's Fish Market down the block at Division and Washtenaw. His question was in Yiddish, for although my grandparents had been in America for 20 years, Harry and Sophie Elkin had no use for this country's tongue.

That day in the store, *Zadie* was dressed in a style closer to the landlady's than the other men. Buttons had fled his shirt, his gray slacks had grease stains from the horse wagon he used for deliveries, and his black suspenders had lost their elastic. When my mother first saw her father in this getup, she said to him, "Mom would *plotz* [explode] if she saw how you left the house."

While I loved my grandparents, I was a little afraid of my *zadie* because of his cloudy right eye. "He was playing with his brother Sam, and didn't duck when Sam threw a knife at him," my mom explained when I first asked about the missing orb.

"You don't need to sell fish," *Zadie* said to my dad, slinging his hand in the air, as if he were swatting a swarm of flies. "If they want fish, they come to me."

His store was also a ground-floor operation with him and *Bubbie* living upstairs, as well as Mom's youngest sister Rose, and her husband, Dave, who was away in the Coast Guard that year. Until they were drafted into the service, Mom's brothers—Carl, Paul, Nate, and Hy—worked in the fish store, too. The Elkin boys had stood behind wooden crates that were filled with crushed ice and dead fish. Lying flat on its side, each fish had a single eye staring up, as unnerving to me as my grandfather's blank eye. The store's customers were Jewish, Polish, and Italian housewives who pointed to whitefish, perch, and trout, then focused on the needle of a bouncing scale, determined to get their money's worth.

That first day in our grocery store, Dad probably didn't want to argue with his strong-as-an-ox father-in-law, who was known to chase his wild sons around the kitchen table with a butcher's knife, but said, "Pa, I'll have to carry some fish—maybe lox, herring, smokefish."

"*Gornish helfn* [what's the use]," *Zadie* answered, shaking his head.

Although I wasn't as fluent as my parents, who had brought the language with them from their Russian *shtetls,* I could *farshtate* much of my grandfather's Yiddish. And because I could understand him, I didn't realize at the time that he was speaking a foreign tongue.

While the two men squabbled, Mom watched from the sidelines, keeping an eye on my brother Ronnie, who was about to pry open the door of the walk-in meat locker. Dressed in a long-sleeved polo shirt, navy pants, and a sailor cap, my older brother was as cute as the kid on the Cracker Jack box.

As for me, a clingy toddler, I was wearing the cotton blouse with Peter Pan collar and red corduroy pants that Mom had chosen for me. I clutched her hand whenever I could, not wanting to lose her among the group touring the store. "My little shadow," she used to say, laughing, when she described me to people. She was right. I stuck close to her because I was less sure of my mother's love for me than my dad's. In my little girl mind, I didn't measure up.

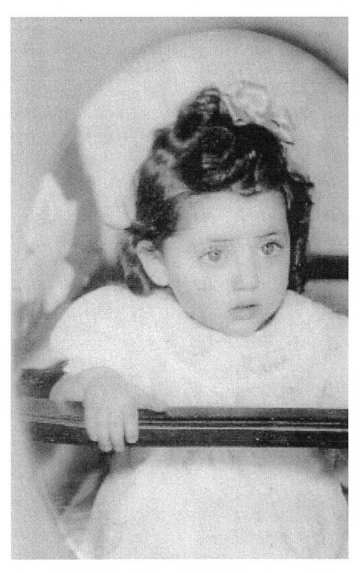

My baby picture mounted on a hand mirror.

I knew I was round-faced like the Shapiros, fixated on food like my father, and cared little for dressing up like Mother. Perhaps I feared she'd leave her second-rate daughter behind if I didn't follow in her high-heeled footsteps.

"Irv, how could we swing the rent on our flat *and* on the store?" Mom asked, her hand nervously squeezing mine.

Zadie interrupted, "*Abi gezunt* [As long as you are healthy]," he said. "If you need . . ." and didn't finish the sentence; he didn't have to. Everyone in the store that day knew that *Zadie* lent money to this one and that one to help him get on his feet, and if his adored *Minkela* needed help, *Zadie* would provide the *gelt*.

"A loan, Pa, only a loan," Dad said, shaking *Zadie's* hand. "We'll pay it back before you know it." Maury and Jack, all smiles, lined up to pound Dad's shoulder and shake his hand, too.

As *mahzel tovs* rang out—especially from a gleeful Mrs. Newman—Dad took Mom away from me and held her two hands in his. "Say yes, honey, please say yes. I know we can make a go of it." My mother sighed and looked at the eager gang who were hanging on her decision, as if she were Snow White and we the giddy dwarfs. "Okay," she said softly.

"Hurray!" Dad yelled. "What should we call it—Min and Irv's Finer Foods? Shapiro's Grocery? What?"

"Irv's Finer Foods. It's your idea, your dream. The store should have your name on it."

Dad hugged Mom, then pulled Ronnie and me into their embrace.

"Yea! This is our store!" I shouted, jumping up to try and kiss Mom's cheek.

"It'll be wonderful," Dad said, drawing my mother closer to him, "just wonderful, I promise."

Like a fox escaping a trap, Mom slipped out of Dad's embrace and turned to watch her overjoyed family. She spread the fingers of her two hands on her thin hips and scanned the store. In voice that did not match ours, she said, "I hope to God you're right."

CHAPTER TWO

One for the Record Books

The Cubs were playing the Giants the day Dad's sister Mary came to our grocery store and begged us to pose for a picture out front. The date was September 29, 1943, and the five-year-old I was back then was torn between leaving the radio broadcast of the game and answering my aunt's request.

I wasn't as nutty a Cub fan as my dad or my 8-year-old brother Ronnie, but because my father brightened when he heard the roar of the Wrigley Field crowd or the crack of a slugger's bat, I came to love the team as well. So on this Wednesday, as soon Jack Brickhouse announced the lineup of Phil Cavaretta, Eddie Stankey, Peanuts Lowrey, Andy Pafko, and other '43 Cubbies, I turned my attention to WGN.

But I also loved my aunt Mary and her request was simple enough—she wanted a black-and-white memento of my family and our corner grocery store, something I'd enjoy seeing, too. Dad's sister, Mary Shapiro Cohen, didn't live on Division Street like the Elkins—my mother's family—but we saw her often. I'm not certain why we weren't as close to Dad's other sister and three brothers, or why we didn't keep in touch when two of them left for Los Angeles and one for Kansas City. Today I wonder: Who dropped the ball—my parents, or Dad's relatives?

What I remember of Dad's sisters and brothers is that Mary, Babe, Jim, and Stash were zaftig and hearty, like Dad; and Ben was slim and serious. In the brief period they were in my life, Dad's family appeared to be fond of my brother and me—possibly because we resembled our father, and because we had a loving relationship with him.

Today I see the absence of the Shapiros as a loss, for I have reconnected with Neil and Gerald—an artist and a

Some of the Shapiros: Dad and his youngest brother Stash are perched on arms of the couch. His two sisters, Mary and Babe, are on either side of Babe's husband, Phil; and Ronnie and I are seated on the floor.

writer—who are the sons of Dad's brother Jim. My two cousins and I share the same Shapiro features, sense of humor, and take on life. And they feel as I do: It was a loss.

On the day Aunt Mary pressed us for the photograph in front of the store, she was wearing a black wool coat over a blue rayon polka-dot dress. I smiled when I saw her because she was a female version of my dad. Sister and brother looked alike: round face, bright brown eyes, and easy smile. Their bodies were similar, too—wider, rather than long. That was another difference between the two sides of my family. Although both the Elkins and the Shapiros came to this country from Russia in the early 1900s, the Elkins remained slim, while the Shapiros seemed to inflate with each year on these shores. And my mother's family quickly got their bearings—finding jobs or starting businesses, while Dad's had harder luck. Did these disparities affect the score between the two families? I'm not certain.

I was hanging out at Dad's counter when Aunt Mary spotted me at the radio. She reached down to give me a bear hug and said, "So, let me see your nails." Earlier that year, in her apartment in an elevator building on Sheridan Road, she had held my chewed fingers in her plump ones and offered to pay me a nickel if I stopped biting my nails. I had eagerly accepted her offer because I wanted the coin. But I was also pleased that she had noticed my hands. Up till then, no one—not even my parents—had mentioned my nervous habit, so I took my aunt's attention as flattery rather than reprimand.

"Look," I said, fanning my undisturbed nails in her

Le Consul de Russie certifie que la photographie et la signature ci-dessus sont celles du titulaire du présent passeport.

Bucarest, le *27 Avril* 1922

LE CONSUL

The Elkin family passport dated April, 1922. Six children are pictured; two more were born in America. My mother, with her beautiful large eyes, is first on the left.

face. On the spot, I won another hug and the promised nickel.

"Irv, come outside," Aunt Mary said, turning to my father. "Hy's waiting with the Brownie."

"A minute, Mary, one minute," Dad said from behind

his meat counter. As he slowed the wheel of his silver slic-
ing machine, pages of pastrami slipped from the sharp,
greasy disk and fell silently on the wax paper below. Just
as he had predicted 18 months earlier, when he first proposed buying the store, Dad had become an enthusiastic
shopkeeper, enjoying his post behind his meat counter
and kibitzing with customers. He was most content when
he could gaze around the space and see Mom, Ronnie,
and me working side by side.

The day of Aunt Mary's visit, Dad was wearing a full-
length, permanently freckled apron over a plaid shirt with
the sleeves rolled up past his wrists. He had clipped dark
blue suspenders to blue slacks that were growing taut
across his paunch.

"Too much, Irv, too much," his customer Mrs. Schwartz
beefed as Dad placed a stack of meat on the Toledo scale.
"You'll make me fat."

"So, what's wrong with fat?" Dad said, reaching over
the deli case to hand her the wrapped package. "A rye to
go with that?" he asked. While he awaited her decision,
he pinched a wedge of halvah from an unwrapped chunk
nearby and tossed it in his mouth.

As I watched Dad's transaction, I thought, Mom's biggest worry came true. Surrounded by food, my father was
steadily expanding, likely adding 20 pounds since the
store's opening day.

I was sympathetic to my father's plight because I also
found it hard to resist the peanut-filled candy bars, va-
nilla ice cream cups with their own tiny wooden spoons,
Kayo chocolate pop, and the extra slices of pastrami that

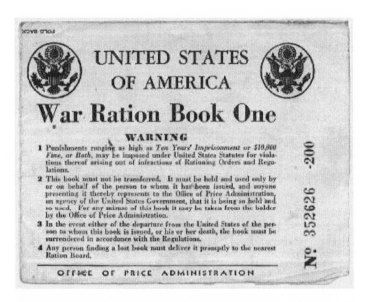

*Copy of a war ration book that our customers used
to purchase certain limited goods.*

customers rejected. All of this free, ever-present food was
Dad's and mine for the taking, if only we could evade
Mom's radar.

While Mrs. Schwartz considered Dad's suggestion
of a rye, she searched her handbag for her ration book.
A *shlumpy* woman who was dressed in a worn woolen
sweater and babushka, Mrs. Schwartz was a steady customer. "Here," she said, "take the red one." A few people
crabbed about the wartime limits on meat, butter, and
sugar; but most, like Mrs. Schwartz, were proudly patriotic
when they redeemed their stamps for scarce provisions.

"Mary, wait until I finish," my mother said to her sister-
in-law who was still seeking the snapshot. "I want to get
rid of the apron."

"No, no, the aprons stay," Aunt Mary said. "I'm sending the picture to the family. I want them all to see how you look in the store. The aprons stay."

Despite the white cloth covering her body, my mother still looked glamorous to me. While my father reveled in his role as butcher, I had the feeling Mom would have preferred dumping her apron and the lowly role it represented. Although she was an able store manager and bookkeeper, I believe—and perhaps she did, too—that those skills would have blossomed in a different setting—an office perhaps, somewhere that didn't require her to stand behind a counter and serve penny-pinching housewives.

On the September day Aunt Mary asked us to pose, Mom had been at her majestic Burroughs cash register with a sharpened pencil tucked behind her ear. Her customer, Mrs. Perelli, was a Gold Star mother, whose son Tony would never return from the Pacific. A woman in her 40s—who looked 10 years older than she'd looked before the grim telegram—took her time settling her grocery selections on the counter.

"Let's see," Mom said, as she flattened a brown paper bag that would serve as calculator and container. She lifted the pencil from its sweet niche, touched and named the Tip-Top sliced bread, Libby's canned peaches, and Chiffon soap flakes, and wrote their prices on the kraft bag.

I loved watching my mom at work, especially when she had to reach items on the highest shelf behind her. She'd take the long grabber pole from its place in the corner, stand on the tiptoes of her high-heeled shoes, and skillfully home in on the can of cut-up pineapple, box of

Wheaties, or other desired item. "Back, back, back. That's it," the customer would yell, as if she were Jack Brickhouse calling a home run. Mom's slim fingers would clamp the pistol-grip handle at the base of the grabber pole, and the two claws at the top would open to swallow the item. Then, squeezing the handle and holding tight, she'd sail the item safely down to the counter. All that was missing when the play ended was Brickhouse's "Hey-hey! Hey-hey!"

Another favorite part was when Mom tallied up the prices of her customer's order in her head. I was impressed with this feat because I had started kindergarten earlier that month and was dazzled to see someone count numbers that fast without an adding machine. My first day in kindergarten at Lafayette Grammar School on Augusta Boulevard had been a strikeout.

I assumed I'd be happy to be in a place full of fresh picture books, boxes of still-pointy crayons in 50 different colors, wooden puzzles with none of their pieces missing, and other five-year-old children. But once I realized Mom intended to leave me behind in that cavernous space with a strange woman, I grabbed my mother's wrist and cried, "Don't go!"

The other children—some of whom were drying their own tears, or were already fighting over toys—stared at me. I remember thinking, I don't care if they call me a baby, I want my mommy.

Fortunately, I survived my mother's leave-taking that first day, and by the end of the week, I was a cheery kindergartner. Now in the store, as I watched my mother chant, "Five, ten, fifteen," and jot columns of numbers on the paper bag, then add the sums in her head, I wondered how many grades at Lafayette would be needed to mimic my mother.

When Mom announced the total, Mrs. Perelli opened her coin purse and said, "Min, I'm a little short today. Can I pay next week?"

My mother shrugged her delicate shoulders, then reached under a shelf to find her black-covered ledger book. She flipped the lined pages and added the day's bill to Mrs. Perelli's packed page.

"You're a doll," Mrs. Perelli said, snapping shut her small, barren pouch.

"Hurry, before the sun disappears," Aunt Mary shouted to her brother, waving a plaid purse she clutched in her hand.

"Hold on, Mary," Dad said. "Pafko's at bat." Andy Pafko had joined the team only five days earlier, and in that game against the Phillies, he advanced his record by driving in four runs with a double and a single in three at bats. The Cubs had won that game 7-4 in a five-inning downpour. On this day, with the Cubs playing the Giants—who we had already beaten three out of four games—the score was tied 3-3.

"We have to wait for Ronnie," Mom said, as she turned her face to the mirror behind her. Dad had hung the glass at Mom's eye level, and now she smoothed her hair from her face and coated her lips with the tube of lipstick she always carried in her skirt pocket. "He'll be back in a minute. He took seltzer up to Mrs. Rubin," she said, patting her upsweep and checking her teeth for red smudges. As I

*Andy Pafko joined the Cubs in 1943. Photo courtesy of
Chicagoland Sports Appearance Connection.*

watched her primp, I felt the same longing as I had when
I caught her performing math: Would I ever be as pretty
as she, or would my best features be folded into flesh like
Aunt Mary's?

"Come, *tsatskele,* come," Aunt Mary called to me in
my sundries section. A few minutes before, I had left the

radio and the Cubs to return to my post because one of my steady customers was there, perusing my stock.

"Sorry to keep you waiting," I said, smoothing my child's-sized apron and imitating my mother's courtesy.

"Go, we'll finish later," Mrs. Levinson said, nudging the small of my back towards Aunt Mary. In her early 30s like my mom, Rose Levinson was also my mother's best friend. If you considered my dark-haired mother to be a double for Dorothy Lamour, then Mrs. Levinson, with her blonde hair pulled back in a French twist, and similarly shapely body, could have been Betty Grable—another popular 1940s pinup.

"No, no," I said to Mrs. Levinson, "let's finish. May I help you, ma'am?" I stood as tall as possible, rising up on the tiptoes of shoes I had tied myself, to grow my shorter-than-average height. Mrs. Levinson played along, pretending as I did, that this miniature store and shopkeeper were the real things.

"I'd like a pack of gum," she said, her hands prim on her purse.

I turned to the shelves that Dad had nailed to the wall and scanned the Ipana toothpaste, Wrigley's gum, Bayer aspirin, and other items that could fit inside my kindergarten-sized palm.

"What flavor?" I asked. "We have spearmint, juicy fruit, and peppermint."

"Spearmint, yes, spearmint," she said after a pause.

"That will be two cents, please," I said, palm out, a satisfied smile on my round face. ("Adorable, like a doll," was how Mrs. Levinson had described my *punim*. "Like a

Shapiro," Mom countered.) When the nickel was pressed into my open hand, I retrieved the desired gum from its spot, then pulled my register from its home on the lowest shelf. Dad had salvaged an empty Muriel Cigar box, painted it white, and loaded it with coins so I could make change. "For you, Princess," he had said when he first presented it to me.

Although I could still make out traces of the lusty Muriel logo winking at me through the paint, and I knew my cash register was a timid imitation of Mom's loud and regal Burroughs, I believed Dad's handiwork to be super, like a line drive with the bases loaded.

The best part of my exchange with Mrs. Levinson came next. "Two cents out of a nickel," I said, lifting copper pennies from their nest in the cigar box. "Three, four, five. One nickel." I dropped each penny into her hand and waited for my reward. "Aren't you the smart one," she said and kissed my cheek.

When the three of us finished taking care of our customers, and Ronnie returned from his delivery, and the Cubs' score was stalled at 3-3, we hustled outside to join Aunt Mary and her husband, Hy Cohen. A genial cigar-smoker, who was a waiter at Joe Stein's Romanian Steakhouse, Uncle Hy was testing sun angles when we emerged from the store.

"No, no, in front of the window," Aunt Mary said. Likely proud of her entrepreneurial brother, she wanted the IRV'S FINER FOODS sign in the shot. But in the black-and-white photo that captured us that day, the sign

Dad's sister Mary with her husband Hy Cohen. Another Hy is off to the side—my mother's youngest brother, Hy Elkin.

is absent. Other advertisements take its place: Ringling Bros. Barnum & Bailey Circus—Now at Soldier Field, Dad's Old Fashioned Root Beer, Rinso White laundry powder, Savoy Foods, and three candy bars: Baby Ruth, Butterfinger, and Jolly Jack.

Of the three confections, Baby Ruth was my dad's favorite. The Curtiss Candy Company developed the log-shaped bar of caramel, peanuts, and chocolate in 1920. It was named either for "Baby" Ruth Cleveland, the first-born daughter of President Grover Cleveland, or baseball slugger George Herman "Babe" Ruth. No matter its provenance, my father lusted for Baby Ruths.

Whenever Mom was busy with customers, or otherwise lax in her surveillance, he would creep to the candy counter and smuggle the forbidden treat. I would often spot him ducking into the bathroom, and knew he was about to gobble the bar and ditch its telltale wrapper. But as always, I never squealed.

On October 17 of that same year, when we were upstairs in our apartment, I heard Dad call out to Mom. "Honey," he said, "come take a look." I remember the date because it was a record-making day for Chicago—it was the same Sunday Mayor Edward J. Kelly officially opened our city's first subway on State Street. When my father heard the ribbon-cutting ceremony on the radio earlier that morning, he said he'd love to live downtown, on State and Madison. I took it to mean that Chicago's busiest corner held a special place in my dad's heart—like the Cubbies and

This photo of officials of the Chicago Rapid Transit Company, representatives of the federal government, and the crew of the eight-car train, was taken April 2, 1943, during the first inspection trip of the State Street Subway. Mayor Edward J. Kelly officially opened the subway October 17 of that same year. Photo by Pete Fish Studios. Courtesy of the Chicago Transit Authority.

Baby Ruth candy bars—all three representing excitement, pleasure, life itself.

Dad was in the bathroom that Sunday when he called out for Mom. Water was running in the tub, and he was undressing for a soak. "Oh my God!" she said, as she pushed open the bathroom door. From my chair in the kitchen, where I had been playing with my Cinderella cut-outs, I could see steam rising from the tub. But the splashing water made it hard to hear more of Mom's words. Startled by Mom's cry, I dropped my cardboard doll and sped towards the bathroom.

"Go away," Mom ordered, shoving me back from the door. But it was too late. I could see Dad with his shoes and socks off, sitting on the edge of the tub cradling his right foot. Instead of five pale toes, Dad held a black mass, as if he had stuck his foot in the stove and got burned.

"Daddy!" I screamed, my heart beating so loud I could hear it in my ears.

Ronnie came running, too. "Yuck!" he said, backing away.

"Go away, kids," Dad said, his voice heavy and unfamiliar.

My brother and I sat cross-legged and silent on the floor outside the closed bathroom door. We heard Mom say she was going to call the doctor—the same one Dad visited when it was time for more insulin. But instead of arranging an appointment for the next day at his office downtown on Wabash Avenue, the doctor insisted Mom take Dad straight to Mt. Sinai, the Jewish hospital on the West Side.

Before leaving the apartment, Mom called her sister Etta to run over and stay with Ronnie and me. When she arrived, Aunt Etta explained that our father had gotten gangrene in his foot and the doctors at Mt. Sinai would clear it up.

"Gangrene?" I said. "But his foot was black, not green."

"It has nothing to do with color, sweetheart," Aunt Etta said, pulling me onto her lap. "It means your daddy got an infected toenail and blood couldn't reach his foot. The bad nail didn't hurt because his diabetes kept him from feeling any pain. The skin on his foot died. That's why it turned black."

"Will my daddy die, too?" I asked, tears starting to fill my green eyes.

"No, *bubbala*, the doctors will fix him up. And if your daddy behaves himself, he'll live a long time."

She was right; Daddy didn't die from the gangrene, although a rabbi did visit his bedside—just in case. The doctors removed the dead tissue on Dad's toes and even saved his foot.

"At first, they thought they'd have to amputate," Aunt Etta told us, her voice shaky, as if she was seeing Dad under the knife. It turned out my father's case made medical history because he was one of the first diabetics to survive gangrene without an amputation.

"They're writing him up in the medical books," Mom said when she returned from the hospital. She also told us that because he was very contagious, she had to put on a smock that was burned after her visit to his room.

When Dad was well enough to get out of his hospital bed and into a wheelchair, Mom took us to visit him. But because we were kids, they wouldn't let us up into his room. So Ronnie and I stood in the hospital's parking lot while Mom pointed up to his window. I think I saw him wave to us, but I'm not sure. No matter. It was enough that my father was getting well, that his diabetes hadn't killed him. He would be coming home, and all would return to normal. What more could a princess hope for?

Dad was supposed to come home on a Friday, but

Mom said the doctors made him stay over the weekend, "to teach him a lesson."

"Your father was very bad," Mom said to Ronnie and me, as she removed her navy wool coat with the padded shoulders and hung it in the hall closet. She closed the mirrored door, and before continuing her story, studied her face. Her makeup was intact, but to me she looked weary, older. Sagging onto a kitchen chair, she said, "After all he went through, after the *tsoris* he put me through, you'll never believe what he did."

Ronnie and I stared at each other. What could our father have done, lying in a hospital bed, that had gotten him into so much trouble?

"There was an orderly, a young man who worked in the hospital and delivered Dad's *Daily News*. Well, your *meshuggana* father bribed the boy to sneak in a pastrami sandwich on rye, two packs of Camels, and three Baby Ruths."

Ronnie and I started to laugh—the image of Dad's triple play comical to the both of us. "It's not funny," Mom said, her eyes pooling with tears. "It's not funny."

We stopped giggling, put our arms around our mother's defeated shoulders, and apologized. "I'm not mad at the two of you," she said. "But your father is going to send me to an early grave." For a second, I worried about Mom's prediction. Both parents on the brink of death? Would I be an orphan, like Annie in the funny papers? But as soon as Mom saw my frightened face—my teary eyes mimicking her own—she lifted me to her lap and kissed me. "I didn't mean it," she said. "I'm just upset. Daddy and I will be around forever."

I was relieved to hear that, and to learn my dad was off the disabled list and would be back behind his meat counter. But I wondered, as I slid under the covers and cradled my stuffed lion like a baby cub, did my father really learn his lesson, or were there more record-breaking days ahead?

CHAPTER THREE

Safe on Our Shores

Summer was the best time to be a kid on Division Street: School was out, daylight stretched past usual bedtimes, best pals lived on the block, and our playground was right outside our front door. True, our concrete field lacked grass or gravel to cushion a fall, and there were no regulation bases or home plates that our neighborhood park offered. But because Humboldt Park was seven blocks away at Sacramento Boulevard, and it was rumored that puny Jewish kids might get hassled by tough Gentiles, my age group stayed close to home.

If a parent, older brother, or group of friends accompanied me to the park, I was happy to go because it had several attributes our sidewalk lacked: lush landscaping, a Prairie-style fieldhouse, a lagoon, rocky brooks, and a rose garden. Also, I was eager to see a statue that stood at the park's entrance that I had grown to love. I had always assumed the couple caught in the granite depicted a mother welcoming home her child. Not until years later did I learn that the sculpture by Charles Mulligan, at the gate of the 207-acre park, was called "Home: The Miner and

41

"Home: The Miner and His Child" is the Humboldt Park
sculpture by Charles Mulligan that I always believed
was a mother welcoming home her child.
Renee S. Elkin Photography.

His Child." It never was a woman waiting for her daughter with open arms.

Unlike Humboldt Park's splendid shade trees, fragrant blossoms, and tranquil waters, our summer backdrop on Division Street consisted of brick apartment buildings, ground-floor businesses with plate glass windows, and cast-iron lampposts. To be heard by playmates, we had to shout above the screeches and horns of passing streetcars and automobiles. And the scents that assaulted our noses were gasoline fumes or cooking odors from open windows in the flats above our heads.

Nonetheless, the kids who lived on busy Division Street, or on nearby side streets like Campbell, Haddon, or Rockwell, considered ourselves charmed in 1944—the year I turned six—to have Chicago sidewalks as our playground.

All sorts of games took place on the hot pavement: Boys hurled pink Spauldings against brick walls to score runs, girls bounced balls and played jump rope and hopscotch, and everyone shot marbles, cast yo-yos, rode secondhand Schwinns, and roller-skated on metal wheels that had to be clamped to our feet.

My child-sized summer seemed to be far from the world events that had gripped our country ever since Japan attacked Pearl Harbor three years earlier. Although I caught bits of news from my parents, or from Movietone newsreels, newspaper headlines, and evening radio broadcasts, I was untouched by the war—like most of my playmates. We knew about D-Day on June 6, 1944, when a million Allied troops under General Dwight D. Eisenhower landed in Normandy. But our families were intact: Our fathers were either too old or unfit, and our mothers sweated in cramped, humble kitchens, or behind store counters. If there was a Rosie the Riveter in my neighborhood, I didn't know her.

Still, I was reminded daily of the war through public-spirited signs that were plastered on Division Street's storefronts, "Buy War Bonds and Stamps. Keep America Free. Let's All Back the Attack With War Bonds." In the comics, Little Orphan Annie urged me to collect scrap metal, Joe Palooka joined the Army, and Terry—of Terry and the Pirates—fought the Japs. And advertisements that my mother read to me from *Life* magazine combined products with patriotism, like the one for the $10 Royal Stetson Playboy hat my father stored on the top shelf of our hall closet: "Loose talk can lengthen the war. So—whatever you hear, whatever you know, whatever you learn, don't let it get to the enemy. *Keep it under your Stetson.*"

Despite these constant cues, I felt safe on our shores, believing my Division Street was a million miles from World War II, a million miles from danger.

In July of 1944, my sidewalk play was simple and cautious because I was small for my age and a poor athlete. I snapped a rubber ball down and up, lifting my right knee as I recited: *A, My Name Is Alice.* My right hand palmed the ball, my left pressed my lightweight cotton skirt flat against my thigh so my underpants wouldn't show. Because of my timidity, I admired girls who were tougher

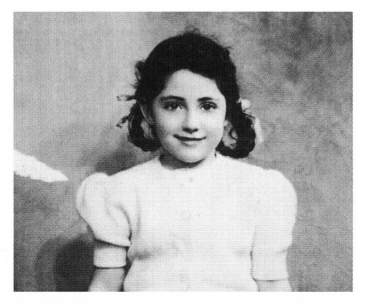

Me in pigtails.

and braver, like Franny Jacobs—or F.J. as she preferred to be called.

"A tomboy, *shmutzik* and wild," my mother had said when I first revealed my reverence for this older girl. I had just come in from playing outside, and Mother was combing my hair with her fingers when she unleashed her criticism, using Yiddish from the old country for emphasis.

"What kind of girl is that? A *mieskeit* [ugly person]. Makes up a name for herself. Does whatever she wants. Oy vey, her poor parents." As my 31-year-old mother used a Kleenex moistened with her saliva to wipe dirt off my face, she went on, "Little girls should act like little girls, not wild Indians."

I hated it when my mother tidied me up like that,

trapping me in her firm hands like a feline pawing her kitten. I suppose I should've been used to it, for that was my mother's reaction whenever she caught me coming in from play. Whether she was downstairs behind the cash register of our grocery store, or upstairs in our flat fixing supper, she'd interrupt her chore to attack my unruly hair and food-spotted mouth. Then, she'd seal my cleansing with, "Stand up straight." What was she grooming me for? I often wondered. If it was to be a glamour girl like her, it was a lost cause.

Just once, I would have loved to have her welcome me with open arms—like the statue in Humboldt Park—instead of with nail-polished fingers poised to rearrange me.

When my mother harped on Frannie Jacobs, I didn't defend or argue, because I was a good little girl who never talked back. Mostly I kept my hero worship to myself. I envied everything about F.J. She was skinny and tall, and nimble like Jane in the "Tarzan" movies. She could outrun any boy on the block, or push back if one were to lay a hand on her. Her wardrobe—untucked shirts and boy's pants—must have been her choosing, unlike the dull matching outfits Mother laid out for me each morning. And F.J.'s sandy-colored hair stood where the wind had styled it. She could hop off her brother's bike without skinning a knee, and if she did scar, she'd display the mark proudly, as if she were a sailor with shore-leave tattoos. And I never saw her cry, not once.

Summer days on Division Street, children claimed

our concrete playing field, but by early evenings, we'd relinquish a portion to our parents. The sidewalk in front
of our store was the customary gathering spot. And since
our block was made up of six- and 12-flat apartment
buildings—absent of porches or stoops—the adults, like
their creative children, improvised.

"Here, put them here," Mrs. Levinson said to her
husband, Saul, one evening that July, as she pointed to a
spot to the right of our grocery's front door. Rose Levinson was the apple of her husband's eye, as well as of her
three sons. Mr. Levinson, bulky like my dad, was schlep-
ping four metal card chairs—two for his wife and him, the
others reserved for my parents.

Although our store usually shut its doors at five—
when my mother flipped the light switch and my father
reversed the "Open" sign—on muggy nights like this one,
they kept the doors unlocked until the last kid had been
dragged upstairs for bed. It was Mom's idea to extend
business hours. "The kids will want ice cream," she said to
Dad. "Why let them get it from the truck?"

My father was 35 years old that year. And although
he was handsome, with a pencil-thin mustache and bright
smile abetted by false teeth, he was unwilling to curb habits that harmed him, like his gluttony and cigarettes.

Despite my mother's prediction about the summer
evening's trade, it was adults, not kids, who would draw
my parents from their seats to buy a bottle of Coca-Cola,
Kayo, or seltzer, or a pack of Chesterfields or Pall Malls.
The kids were like Alan Levinson, who was tugging on his

father's shirt and hopping up and down at the sound of the Good Humor bell. "Pa, it's coming!" Alan screamed. "I need two cents."

As Mr. Levinson reached into his trouser pocket for loose change, Mrs. Levinson turned to my mother, put a hand on Mom's aproned knee, and said, "Min, I'm sorry."

"Don't worry," my mother said, waving away her friend's apology. "Let him enjoy."

But when Mom saw Alan return from the white truck, with a Toasted Almond Bar in one hand, and a Push-Up in the other, then watched several more neighborhood kids duplicate his purchase, her face grew dark and troubled. Her expression reminded me of the time I had overheard my parents discussing Hitler, concentration camps, and gas chambers. When I had asked them what they were talking about, they said I was too young to hear such things. It had something to do with Jews, that much I knew; but Hitler was far, far away, where the war was, so I dropped my interrogation.

On that July evening, the Friedmans and the Rosenbergs soon joined the Levinsons on the sidewalk. Each newcomer carried a card chair that squeaked as it was unfolded. These were the same chairs that were stored flat in a hall closet, then opened weekly for rounds of pinochle and gin rummy, or canasta and kalukee. This night, as our neighbors settled in on their metal chairs, the men unbuttoned shirt collars and lit unfiltered cigarettes, and the women fixed their eyes on their wild *kinderlach* on the concrete stage before them.

Some of the men debated Friday night's wrestling matches at Marigold, "Whadda you talking? *Feh*, Gorgeous George is a fake, he couldn't pin my *bubbie* to the mat. Chief Don Eagle, now that's a wrestler." I heard some of the men talking about the Democratic National Convention that was held in Chicago on July 20. "That's good for the Jews," Mr. Levinson said. "A fourth term for Roosevelt, and Truman for vice president instead of Wallace."

"And the Democratic and Republican parties both agreed Palestine should be for the Jews, what about that?" Mr. Friedman said. "That's even better for us."

"Did you hear a German colonel tried to assassinate Hitler?" Mr. Rosenberg asked. But as soon as he spotted me eavesdropping, he changed to another topic—the Cubs, I think.

A few of the men, including my father, shunned chit-chat and folded damp arms under heads, and leaned back against the brick building. Subdued by a day of labor, several helpings of heavy Jewish cooking, and gasoline fumes from the street, they *schloffed*. Nothing could rouse our dozing fathers—neither the screams of their flying children, nor the sounds of radio programs that leaked from open windows overhead. The crackly broadcasts of *The Goldbergs* or *The Jack Benny Show*, with their familiar characters and easygoing plots, lulled—rather than disturbed—the drained men.

This particular evening, my mother was unfolding a flimsy blue envelope and reading news of her four brothers who were stationed overseas. "Listen," she said, pulling on her girlfriend's bare arm to catch her attention. "You'll never believe what my brother Nate did. He's in the Army Engineers, you know." Then, she smoothed the airmail letter in her lap and read: "One of my pals told me he had seen a guy named Elkin in a military hospital, and that the soldier had malaria. I figured it was our brother Carl, because I hadn't heard from him in a few weeks." As my mother continued Uncle Nate's airmail, Mrs. Levinson's eyes darted from my mother's face to her kids'—as if she was watching a tennis match at Humboldt Park. When the ball returned to Mom's court, she read on: "So I went AWOL until I found Carl. The docs said he's okay, just resting up till they send him home. But guess where I am?" Mother paused here for dramatic effect. When Mrs. Levinson failed a guess, Mom read, in a loud voice mixed

The youngest Elkin boy, Hy,
in his sailor uniform.

with humor and surprise: "In the brig! I have to serve seven days, one for each day I was gone from my outfit."

With my mother wrapped up in her brother's letter, and my father out for the count, I joined a game of ring-a-levio in progress. Richie Freedman was "It." He was leaning into the lamppost, eyes closed, and counting to 100. Like the rest of the gang, I ran to hide, and picked the passageway between our apartment building and the next. Although it was dark in there, I wasn't scared because I could hear Richie's loud count, and the rise and fall of adult voices. When Richie yelled, "Olie Olie Ocean Free," we all leapt from our hiding places and raced to touch the metal post before Richie could tag us.

As I sped to the goal, I pretended I was my hero F.J., or Jane in the jungle, free and fearless, flying through the air on a ropy vine. With Tarzan's imagined yell trumpeting in my ears, I turned my hands into fists and pumped my small arms as hard as I could.

But as I neared the post, Alan Levinson came flying in from another direction. Like fighter planes in the newsreels, the ones that exploded in midair combat, Alan and I smashed into each other and fell backwards to the merciless pavement. As we lay groaning, our mothers sprung from their chairs and sped to our splayed bodies.

I tried to hold back tears as my mother inspected my arms and legs. *"Meshugganas,"* she said, after assuring there were no broken bones. "That's what you get for playing rough." Then, after performing her on-the-spot cleanup and pocketing the used Kleenex, she kissed my forehead and returned to her chair. Afterwards, I wore my Mercurochromed bruises proudly, unlike some of the other scars I collected later that week on Division Street.

Several days after the accident, on a Friday, I was healed and roller-skating in front of our store. Since none of my friends were around, I decided to skate to Deborah Boys Club and wait for my nine-year-old brother, Ronnie. Deborah was a Jewish community center just a half block east of our store, across Campbell Avenue. When my brother was not busy delivering groceries, he spent as much time as he could at the club. Short for his age, too, Ronnie was athletic and cute. Although his eyes weren't blue like my mother's, and he had a *punim* more like the Shapiro side of the family, Ronnie was my mother's Jewish prince. While I sometimes longed for the same delight she granted him, most of the time, I wasn't jealous because I was crazy about my big brother, too.

Before leaving for Deborah, I rolled inside the store to tell my mother my plans. "Be careful crossing the street," she said, glancing up from her sales counter and customer, "and come straight home for supper."

"Okay," I said. I skated away, singing the "Mairzy doats" song and pretending I was Sonja Henie and the sparkles below my skates were imbedded in ice, not concrete.

As I was ready to perch on Deborah's front steps, I brushed the stone with a Kleenex. Although I was wearing playclothes, I knew Mother wouldn't like it if I got them dirty. Then, I removed the skate key that hung from a string around my neck and unscrewed the metal frames that were fastened tight to my summer sandals.

A man I never saw before approached. He was wearing a brown suit, white shirt, fat brown tie, and brown Stetson, and he looked like the man in the newsreels at the Vision Theater down the block at Washtenaw. Every Saturday afternoon, before the Lone Ranger serial or Porky Pig cartoon, the man on the movie screen spoke into a round microphone and told us about our boys in their dive bombers fighting the Germans and the Japs.

"Aren't you a cutie," the man I never saw before said. He was bending down on one knee to get closer.

"Thank you," I said, not surprised by his compliment. Lots of people told me I was cute—with my peewee body, green eyes, and wavy black hair.

"Would you like to see my dolly?" the man asked in a soft voice, smiling like my dad did when we played *Which Hand Has the Penny?*

"Where is it?" I asked, stacking my skates on top of each other.

"Come on, I'll show you," he said, reaching for my hand.

I thought about the doll I had at home. She had brown-lashed eyes that could roll open. Without her dress, Elizabeth's gray muslin body looked dull. Her arms and legs were hard and the color of Cheerioats.

Maybe the man's doll would be wearing a purple velvet coat with lace at the wrists, like the one inside a box in Neisner's store window. The box had a cellophane cover, so you could see the doll inside if you passed by, but she wouldn't get soiled waiting for someone to buy her.

I looked to the door of Deborah, but Ronnie was not

coming out. Although I didn't know the man kneeling before me, he seemed nice—just like all the men on my block whose names I knew well. My mother had warned me about looking both ways before crossing Campbell, but she said nothing about friendly men who promised a peek at a doll. So I forgot about my brother, gathered the skates in the crook of my left arm, and put my right hand in his. I was surprised: The man's hand felt sweaty, as if he had washed up and forgotten to use a towel.

We walked just a few feet, to a passageway that separated the boys' club from its neighboring building. Although people passed us by, I didn't recognize any of them. And they probably didn't realize that this placid, smiling couple holding hands on Division Street was not a father and daughter out for an afternoon stroll.

I didn't like the passageway he took me into, and I wondered why this nice man picked this dusty place to show me his doll. It was dark inside there, and it smelled like the garbage Daddy put out in the back of our store at closing time. My sleeveless blouse and shorts brushed against the brick wall, and I was worried there would be dirt marks. But still, there was going to be a doll.

"Where's the dolly?" I asked, when we stopped walking and he turned to face me.

"Right here," he said. "You can touch it." He unbuttoned and unzipped his pants, like I'd seen my daddy do when he was getting ready for bed. But then the man put his hand in his pants and lifted out—what? Something ugly, scary, but definitely not the dolly I was expecting.

He took my hand from where it was stuck to the side

of my body and placed it on the nasty fat, pink tube that was poking outside his pants. The glistening thing, that was definitely not a dolly, felt and smelled like the rubber gloves my mother wore at the kitchen sink.

I didn't like his hand on mine. I didn't like the way my body was feeling. My stomach tightened, like it did in the movies when B-17s roared across the screen, or when we had duck-and-cover air raid drills in school. I wanted out of this scary passageway with this man who tricked me. I wanted to go home. I began to wail—surprisingly loud sobs for such a peanut.

This is a bad man, I thought to myself. Now he's made me do something bad, too. I shouldn't have gone with him. I should have punched him in the nose, like F.J. would've done. I should've yelled as loud as Tarzan. But I was a fraidy cat after all. Now all I could do was weep.

"Sshh, stop crying," the man said, his voice gruff. "I didn't hurt you, you little baby. You're okay."

He was right, he didn't hurt me. But somehow, I felt dirty and it wasn't just the *schmutz* that had gotten on my clothes. I worried that Mommy and Daddy would be mad at me for not waiting for Ronnie—mad at me for doing a bad thing. While I continued to cry, the man hid the tube back in his pants, buttoned and zipped his trousers, and took my hand to lead me out of the passageway. I cradled the roller skates close to my body with my other hand, as if the skates were my doll Elizabeth, the doll I now loved so much, the faithful one waiting for me on my bed.

"Go home," he said, giving my shoulder a shove to-wards the boys' club. He turned and walked quickly away in the other direction. But I didn't want to wait for Ronnie anymore. I wanted my Mommy and Daddy. I ran—as fast as I did in ring-a-levio, imagining the sidewalk to be the soft spongy floor of the jungle, instead of Division Street's harsh concrete.

When I reached our store, the lights were out, and that meant my parents were now upstairs in our apartment. Mommy would be cooking dinner, while Daddy would be collapsed in his sagging armchair. The *Chicago Daily News* would be spread open on his lap—its pages being flipped by the electric fan near his chair—but Daddy's brown eyes would be closed, his head pasted back, and his mustached-mouth open and snoring.

Still gripping my skates and still crying, I pushed open the door to our apartment and slammed into my mother. With my teary face flat into her apron, I told her about the man, the missing doll, and the awful pink pipe. Like the sculpture in the park, my mother opened her arms wide for me, and never once tried to clean my face or comb my hair. Instead, she cried, too. When our noise woke my dad, he listened to my story, then rushed to the phone.

Who was he calling? I wondered. Why were they both so angry? I didn't ask these questions because I relished Mom's tight embrace and didn't want to upset my parents any further. I figured I had done enough for one evening.

"We're going downstairs, sweetheart," Mother said, taking my hand.

When we got to the street, a policeman told Mom and me to get in the back seat of his patrol car while Dad sat in the front. "Tell me if you see the man who promised you a doll," the policeman said to me. "Take your time, honey."

I sat on my mother's lap as the policeman drove the blue-and-white patrol car slowly up and down the streets and through the neighborhood alleys. The roads were quiet. All of my friends must have been upstairs in their apartments eating supper, or maybe listening to Kate Smith sing "When the Moon Comes Over the Mountain" on the radio.

Without the giddy noise of my playmates, without the watchful eyes of our parents, this summer night on Division Street looked foreign, sinister. Although I did as I was told, and searched for the man in the brown fedora, the brown suit, and the fat brown tie, I couldn't find him.

After awhile, after shaking my head "no" to the policeman's, "Is that him? What about him?" whenever we spotted a man walking alone, the officer brought us back to our apartment building.

"Sorry, we didn't see him tonight," he told my parents, "but we'll keep our eyes open for the son of a bitch."

When Ronnie arrived home, Dad took him out in the hallway on our floor. "If I ever see him, I'll kill him," I could hear my big brother shout outside the door.

"My blouse and shorts got dirty," I said to my mother, as she helped me into the bathtub later that night. "I brushed off the step at Deborah before I sat down, but dust from the wall got on me anyway."

"Don't worry, honey, don't worry," she said, as she lathered flowery-smelling pink Camay on my body. "It'll come out in the wash." I knew my mother meant the clothes I wore that day, but I hoped she could also scrub the dirty feeling from my body.

After the next washday, there were my blouse and shorts folded on my bed, along with socks, pajamas, and other laundry. The playclothes I wore that summer day in 1944 were clean as could be. Not a mark on them, just like Mother had promised.

My parents never explained what had happened to me in the passageway, or why little girls should be wary of strangers, just like they are of cars when they cross the street.

Perhaps—like their conversations about Hitler, camps, and gas—my mother and father believed I was too young to hear such things. Maybe they thought if we didn't discuss the brown-suited man, the promised dolly, the dark passageway, the ugly pink tube, and the ride in the patrol car, the incident would be forever erased from my mind, and I would feel safe once again on Division Street.

CHAPTER FOUR

Gonna Take a Sentimental Journey

On April 12, 1945, people poured onto Division Street to share their grief when they learned President Roosevelt had died. And on May 8, the same throng—now jubilant and grateful—filled the streets to celebrate the Allies' victory over Nazi Germany. That mixture—of crying one day and horn blowing the next—seemed to repeat itself throughout that year, though at times, light came before dark.

In the fall of that roller coaster year of highs and lows, Cub fans were ecstatic on September 29th when we clinched the National League pennant by beating the Pittsburgh Pirates. But our cheers turned to gloom October 10th after losing the World Series to the Detroit Tigers—our seventh consecutive series loss.

Similarly, my family's first trip to the country—to Union Pier, Michigan—a resort town 90 miles southeast of Chicago—would be remembered lopsided: some scenes fondly recalled, others melancholy. The idea of a summer in the country was hatched in May, 1945, shortly after V-E Day, when I was seven years old. I was in the kitchen upstairs when my mother's sister Mollie presented the plan. My aunt was exhilarated because the war's end meant their four brothers would soon be returning home.

"Come with us to the country," Aunt Mollie said to my mother, as she unfolded and flattened a brochure on our Formica kitchen table. "*Lantsmen* from my Workmen's Circle have been going to Union Pier for the past few summers, and they tell me more and more Jewish people come every year. We'll split the rent on a few cabins and get away from the city—from the noise, the dirt. Look, paradise," she said, pointing to the full-color photos.

I knew the Workmen's Circle did good things for Jewish people: They were passionate about politics, helped greenhorns get apartments, and tried to raise the minimum wage above $0.40 an hour. If Workmen's Circle members liked Union Pier, it must be a special place, I thought.

At the time of Aunt Mollie's visit, I was curled on the living room couch, twirling a lock of hair with one hand and turning the pages of *Hansel and Gretel* with the other. This was one of my favorite Grimm Fairy Tales, although I often wondered why the authors used a delectable cookie house to lure innocent children. After all, food was a high point in my young life, especially sweets. Why mix my heart's desire with peril? When I was two, and my mother first read the story to me, I was frightened of the old witch and her evil scheme to fatten the children and eat them. But now, with an "E+" in reading on my report card, I could follow the tale myself. I knew the wicked witch would die, and Hansel and Gretel would survive and never return to their cruel mother, who abandoned them in the

Aunt Mollie in her volunteer Red Cross uniform.

forest. The youngsters would live happily ever after with their loving father.

Although I was caught up in Hansel and Gretel's drama, when I heard Aunt Mollie describe Union Pier, I turned my book upside down to save my place and ran to the table.

"Let me see, too," I pleaded, pushing myself between the sisters' bent-over blouses.

"The kids will love it," Aunt Mollie said to my mom. Then she pinched me on the cheek and kissed the bruise. Despite the tweak, I adored this slim, dark-haired aunt, just like I did all of my mother's sisters and brothers. It wasn't only because they beamed when they saw me—and never once criticized my messy hair or pudgy waist—but my mother seemed to perk up in their presence. Although she was the third oldest in a family of eight children, my 32-year-old mother was treated as if she was the most favored—the one most likely to lead a fairy-tale life.

"They'll have their cousins to play with and won't have to ride two streetcars to get to the beach," Aunt Mollie said. She was dressed in a white blouse with padded shoulders, a gray cotton skirt; and she wore high-heeled shoes like my mom did. But unlike my mom, my aunt never wore a grocery store apron. Her husband, Jack Silver the fruit peddler, was a good provider. Aunt Mollie didn't need to work for a living.

"And, you can forget about *meshugganas* on the street," Aunt Mollie said. "Irv can take care of the store by himself. He'll come out on weekends like the other husbands.

Etta, Rose, and their kids will be there. If the boys are back from the service by then, they'll come, too. Say 'yes,' you need the break."

While my mother took a slow sip of coffee and contemplated her sister's sales pitch, I studied the brochure and pictures. I read the words I knew, sounded out the rest, and used my index finger to track the letters: "Fresh air, rustic cottages with outdoor showers, night skies filled with stars, and a short walk down a wooden stairway to an endless, clean sandy beach. A Paradise of Peace and Quiet . . ."

"Mommy, Mommy, please let's go," I begged, yanking on my mother's arm. She freed the brochure from my fingers and turned me towards the living room a few feet away. "Go back to your book," she said, giving my *tush* a pat. "Let me finish talking with Aunt Mollie."

"I don't know if Irv can handle the store alone," my mother said, when she was certain I was back on the couch and into my book. But as soon as Mom's head was turned, I eavesdropped and sneaked peeks at the table and the two sisters. From the corner of my eye, I could see Mom lift a piece of strudel from a pan she had taken out of the oven before Aunt Mollie arrived.

I had hatched a plan when I first saw Mom prepare her famous strudel. From the moment she put on her puffy, stained mitts to remove the fragrant pan from the red-hot oven, I wanted to grab a piece for myself. But I remembered the gingerbread house and Hansel and Gretel's plight, so I waited. I knew I'd never suffer the children's punishment, but I could surely count on a slap on my fingers and Mom's, "You don't need that." So I stayed put, but didn't forget the strudel.

"It's not the store you're worried about," Aunt Mollie said, as she also took a piece of the pastry. "Irv will behave himself. He knows you mean business."

"What about Coffee and Major?" my mother said, tearing her strudel in two, and popping half in her mouth.

"I thought you told me that *dreck* was finished."

"Yeah, the police closed them down and Irv promised no more. But who knows, maybe with me out of town, they'll be back."

I knew what Mom was talking about, and for a moment, my mind wandered from the Elkin sisters at the kitchen table to a pleasant memory of Coffee and Major, the neighborhood bookies who often visited us in the kitchen in the rear of our grocery store. Major—fat and gigantic, and an Oliver Hardy look-alike—would prepare delectable scrambled eggs. He'd crack a handful into a huge mixing bowl (at $0.64 a dozen, Mom kept an eye on his take), add some secret spices, then toss the mixture into a sizzling cast-iron frying pan. Coffee, his partner in crime and culinary, was the thin, nervous Stan Laurel of the duo. He brewed his namesake drink while we all waited hungrily for the crooks' dish.

I also knew why Mom was worried about Dad and the bookies, for I had learned details just the week before when my parents' loud voices awakened me from sleep.

"A hundred bucks a week," my dad had said. "We

can't throw that away." I heard the click of glass, likely an ashtray, then smelled cigarette smoke, and knew my dad would be lighting up one of several Camels.

"I don't care what he gives you. I don't want a bookie joint in the back of my store," Mother had said. "Even if it's after we close up." She was moving around the kitchen, the sound of her wedge houseslippers mingling with the *swish-swish* of a broom across the linoleum.

A bookie joint! I projected a scene straight out of the movies: Jimmy Cagney types in wide-shouldered suits and dark fedoras, banks of ringing telephones, cigar smoke, stacks of cash.

"Whadaya worried about?" my father had said, interrupting the film I was directing.

"The police, like the last time." My mother's voice had risen as the sweeps came faster and louder.

Police! There were police in our store! I leapt from my bed and opened the bedroom door several inches wider, anxious not to miss a word. This was better than *The Adventures of Sam Spade* or *The Inner Sanctum*—two of our favorite radio programs.

"That was *bupkis*," Dad had said laughing. "Major paid off the cops like always, but some *schmuck* thought he'd make detective if he blew the whistle."

"I was never so ashamed in my life. My own husband getting shoved into a patrol car. Neighbors hanging from the windows, watching you get dragged off to jail. Tell me that was nothing. Tell me that was good for business."

Jail! My daddy was in jail! How did I miss this? Did

Ronnie know? I looked over at my 10-year-old brother, who was fast asleep and lightly snoring on his side of the bed. Suddenly it was quiet in the kitchen, and I imagined my mother had abandoned her broom to flop onto a kitchen chair.

In my film, my father would have put his strong arms around his wife's thin shoulders to accompany the reassuring dialogue I had actually heard him say, "I was out of jail the same night. Major took care of it. No big deal."

My mother had started to cry, then Dad said, "Please, sweetheart, stop. I promise. No more bookies." Did my father kneel and kiss both of her work-weary hands? Did my mother return his kiss? That's what I would have directed my actors to do. But in the real-life scene taking place on the other side of the bedroom door—the one starring my parents and not Hollywood sweethearts—I was pretty sure nothing like that was going on.

"You worry too much," Aunt Mollie said to my mother at the kitchen table. Her voice woke me from my daydream, and I quickly turned my attention back to Union Pier.

My mother sighed, rose from her seat, and hoisted the aluminum coffeepot from the stove. She refilled two chipped coffee cups and pushed a bowl of sugar and bottle of cream towards her sister.

"It's easy for you, Mollie," Mother said, vigorously stirring her coffee so that some of the hot liquid spilled to the table. "Jack is a worker. He doesn't mess around with *goniffs* [thieves], or go to the poolroom like my husband.

Jack brings his money home to you each night." Mother then reached behind her, snatched a dishrag from the sink, and wiped up the spill.

Oy vey, the poolroom, that could be another of my 36-year-old father's kicks that could keep us from Union Pier. How was it, I wondered, that something my father found so pleasurable, could irritate my mother and disturb me so much? The poolroom was in a plain storefront that sat in the middle of our block. Except for a small dusty window with an unlighted Humboldt Billards neon sign, you couldn't tell what went on inside.

All of the other stores along the street flaunted huge plate glass windows and displayed merchandise that lured shoppers in. But the poolroom looked sinister, dark, as if its goings-on couldn't stand the light of day.

I never willingly entered the place, but occasionally Mom would ask me to go there and bring Dad home for supper. It wasn't the other men who hung out at the place that I was shy about—guys who rumpled my head—like my young uncles who joined Dad for pool or cards before they were drafted, or the other men whom I knew from the neighborhood.

The disturbing part about the poolroom were the Varga Girl calendars tacked on every wall. These pictures of blonde-haired beauties, with torsos that stretched from the top of the calendar to the page of the month, pulled my eyes towards them the moment I entered the smoke-filled room. Although *Miss February* might dangle a sheer scarf from a manicured hand, or *Miss July* would use a wide-brimmed hat to mask her anatomy, my youthful eyes would be dragged to the perfect breasts of these painted ladies.

I thought about the last time I was there, just a few days before Aunt Mollie's visit. On that occasion, I had entered the poolroom's front door, my eyes searching through the cigar and cigarette haze until I heard, "It's my princess. One minute, one minute, sweetheart. Let me finish the hand." The sound of Dad's voice had broken the calendars' hold and I took a seat at an empty card table, pushed away a butt-filled ashtray, and waited. My dad was wearing a short-sleeved white shirt, his bloodied butcher's apron abandoned in the store. His left arm was oddly tanned, fingers to elbow, a weird stain from hanging his arm out the window on Sunday drives. Like he did at home, here at his spot in the poolroom, Dad had unclasped his belt buckle, released his pants' zipper, and pushed his card chair a few inches from the table's edge.

I had stared at his paunch, which was occupying the space between him and the table, and thought how alike my father and I were in our love of food. Was it simple appetite that attracted us to desserts and deli? Or, having been served a helping of mother's love we found skimpy, did we turn to food to fill us up?

The poolroom smelled stale, damp, and smoky; and it was loud. A radio dial was turned to the baseball scores and met by occasional shouts of, "Those *momsers* [bastards]!" I could hear calls of "Gin!"—and the slap of playing cards against the metal tables, and the pings of billiard balls as they batted into each other. Someone whose poker hand had just been bested, let out "Son of a bitch!" then halted in midair as he glanced in my direction. "Oh, sorry, honey, forgive my big mouth," he had said. Finally, Dad zipped up his trousers, buckled the belt, scooped a handful of coins from the middle of the card table into his pocket, and rose from his seat. "Okay, Princess, let's go home," he had said, lifting my hand to his lips for a kiss, then sealing the same hand into his moist palm.

"Promise me you'll think it over," Aunt Mollie said to Mom, interrupting my memories. As their chairs scraped away from the table, I watched Mom put the coffee cups in the sink, brush strudel crumbs into the garbage pail, and turn on the faucet to rinse the plates.

"I will, I will," she said to her sister, kissing her cheek. Turning to me, she ordered, "Come, I'm going back down to the store."

"Can I stay and finish my book?" I asked. "Only a few more minutes."

"Okay, but hurry up."

But instead of returning to the couch and the Brothers Grimm—and with my warden out of the picture—I could follow the aroma of baked dough, sweetened apples, and bite-sized walnuts that would lead to my treat. I could devour the plump strudel alone now, undetected, in secret.

That same night, in the middle of my usual star light, star bright prayer, I heard my parents discussing Aunt

Mollie's Union Pier idea. As I had done during their earlier bookie joint conversation, I took a seat on the bedroom floor, opening the door wider.

"You should go," I could hear Dad say. "You'll be with your sisters, and you won't have to worry about the kids every minute."

"So, I'll worry about you instead."

"I'll be okay. I can take care of myself."

"No *chazeray* [junk food]?"

"I promise," Dad said. "No candy bars, no corned beef sandwiches."

"No bookies? No betting at the poolroom?"

There was silence, and I assumed my dad was nodding "yes," for my mother continued, "And you'll take care of the bills while I'm gone? The Savoy driver said no more deliveries if we don't pay."

"I'll pay, I'll pay." Dad was yawning now. I could hear the thud of the Murphy bed as it landed on our living room carpet. With their conversation over, I stayed on the bedroom floor, my folded arms and my face resting on my drawn-up knees. I fantasized about Union Pier and the Paradise of Peace and Quiet we'd find there. I'd miss my dad, that was for sure, and I'd worry about him in Chicago without us. But I liked the idea of more time alone with Mom.

Maybe, without the aggravation of the store and worries over my dad's bad habits, she'd be sunnier. Perhaps she wouldn't pack her daily demands of "comb your hair," "stand up straight," or "you don't need that." Maybe in Union Pier—happy to be with her adored sisters—she'd like me just the way I was.

And so, on Saturday, August the 4th, my parents closed our grocery store early for the trip to Union Pier. Dad piled us, and Aunt Etta's family, into his Buick Roadster for the four-hour drive. (A speeder, Dad predicted he'd make it in three.) I sat up front with Uncle Maury, who did not drive or own a car. I won the window seat, "because Dad couldn't say 'no' to his princess," my brother snickered. My mom, Aunt Etta, Ronnie, and my younger cousins David and Estherly filled the back seat. It was the same seating arrangement as on Sunday outings when Dad would chauffeur the two families to Pekin House on Devon Avenue for chop suey and egg foo young, or to a Dairy Queen in *kishneff* (far-flung) for chocolate-dipped cones.

As we drove Route 12 that took us around Lake Michigan, Aunt Etta—possibly to divert us from the stench of the Gary, Indiana, steel mills—started to sing the lyrics to "Sentimental Journey," just like Doris Day. By the time my blonde-haired aunt reached the third verse, we were all bellowing the final words. When we arrived in Union Pier, silly from our song, the four kids tumbled out of the car and raced to the cabins that Aunt Mollie had leased. Although this simple place in the country hardly matched its glowing brochure, it was green enough to make me feel as if I had landed in the middle of Humboldt Park. Tall trees framed the small cottages, and I could smell the pure lake waters nearby.

Except for the whoops of greeting cousins and the crunch of Dad's Buick on the gravel, there was hardly a sound.

Mom's sister Etta caught by surprise.

We left our suitcases unpacked, but plucked out our bathing suits. Then we ran inside to change out of the clothing that had dampened and clung to our bodies during the long, steamy ride. Suited, we raced to the dune steps that led to the lake—where the scene was similar to North Avenue Beach back in the city—only a lot fewer people. Adults were lying flattened on blankets or spreading baby oil on one another's backs. Small children squatted at the water's edge and used plastic pails and shovels to build sand castles, or bury an obliging parent. Older kids were farther out in the water, some riding a friend's shoulders and trying to toss a similar jockey into the surf. This was Paradise, I thought, just like the brochure had promised.

On Sunday night after supper, all of the fathers prepared to leave their families in the country and return to jobs in the city. As I stood on the running board of my dad's car to get one last kiss, I said, "Please take care of yourself, Daddy. Pretty please."

"I promise, Princess," he said, one hand on the ignition key, the other on the steering wheel. "See you next Saturday." Ronnie threw him a wave, then ran to catch up with some 10-year-olds he had met on the beach. My mother, who had said her good-byes to Dad earlier, waved, too. Throw him a kiss, I silently urged. But instead, she stared at my father as if she could see right through him—all the way back to Division Street. Her arms were crossed in front of her, and she was hugging her thin body, as if the summer sun had failed to reach her.

The next day, without our fathers, was Monday, August 6th, and also my cousin Estherly's sixth birthday.

On the same day that the Elkin sisters and their children were sprawled on the placid sands of Lake Michigan—and I was fantasizing about the cake and ice cream that would be served with supper—a United States B-29, the *Enola Gay,* was dropping an atomic bomb on Hiroshima.

When we learned the news from an arriving sunbather who had just heard it on her cabin radio, the children in the brilliant sunshine of Union Pier cheered our country's military might. "Kaboom!" my brother said, and threw the biggest stone he could find into the lake to create a splash. My Aunt Mollie hugged each one of her sisters. "Now all the boys will come home," she said. "Next summer, they'll be here, too." She was smiling with her prediction, as if she could already see her four brothers and their sweethearts sunning themselves on the sand.

We repeated our first day's beach routine throughout the following week. When the sun lowered into Union Pier's lake, the Elkin sisters and their children slogged back up the rickety stairway to the cabins. We schlepped blankets, beach balls, and inner tubes—which seemed weightless on the way down, but were leaden on the long trudge up. And we took turns at the outdoor showers, washing sand off pained, sunburned bodies. Then, dressed in clean playclothes, the children drooped on fiery enameled lawn chairs or striped canvas deck chairs while our mothers patted raw ground beef into hamburgers, or snipped plump Vienna hotdogs from a link which they dropped onto sizzling grills. The schedule changed only on rainy days, when the beach was off limits. Then, we'd stay indoors and play endless rounds of Monopoly, or read comic books we bought on trips to town.

At night, all of the children slept on army cots that were spread throughout the cottages. I remember bumping into snoring bodies on my way to the single bathroom, and wiping ever-present sand off my bare feet before returning to bed.

Sometimes, I'd think about my dad and find it hard to fall asleep. Despite the clean air, family playmates, and

Mom's sister Rose with her husband, Dave Levy.

Mom's sweeter disposition, I often hungered for home and Division Street's characters and clamor. At times, the long days outdoors and unchanging routine bored me. And at night, without street lamps to light our path, I thought the woods too dark and scary.

Often, I had the same dream: My parents had divorced, and my father was living alone somewhere. Like Gretel in the fairy tale, I longed for my father and searched for him among the faces that passed me by. Finally, I'd spot him sitting at a third-floor window, smoking a cigarette and staring at the pitch-black sky.

"Daddy," I would call up to him in my dream. "Look, it's me, your princess. I'm down here." But he didn't see or hear me. He just blew smoke rings and gazed into the dark. Every time I'd have that nightmare, I'd wake up trembling.

One Saturday afternoon, a few weeks after we first arrived in Union Pier, I left the beach early so I could greet my father. I jumped up and down as I watched Dad pull up in his Buick. Before he had a chance to unfold himself from the driver's seat, I hopped on the running board and, through the open window, kissed his sweaty, whiskered cheek. He was rumpled and covered in cigarette ash, but I couldn't care less.

"Princess, I missed you," he said panting, as he exited the car and lifted me in the air. "Are you having fun? You're so lucky to be here, away from the *shvitzing* city."

"I missed you, too, Daddy," I said, happy to hug him and relieved to feel him alive, still my father, still married to my mother. He was right here in the flesh, where I could scrape my face against his stubble, smell his salami-and-tobacco breath, and touch his muscled, sunburned arm.

On the day I ran to meet him, Dad went into the cabin to catch a nap before the clan returned from the beach. He must have heard my mother's voice, because when she came near the screen door, I saw him rush out and smooth his wrinkled clothes as he moved towards her.

"Honey," he said, "come give me a kiss. Did you miss me?"

"I'm a mess," Mom said, backing away from him and covering her bathing suit with the beach towel she was carrying. "Let me clean up first."

That evening, with the chirping of crickets outside, my parents were in the bedroom behind the skimpy closed door and I could hear Dad still asking for his welcome-home kiss.

Then the explosion began. "Don't lie to me," my mother was saying. "I know the bookies came back. Jack heard it on the street and told Mollie." There was no response from Dad, so Mom pressed on: "Did you pay the Savoy driver, or did you throw the money away in the poolroom?"

And finally from my dad a second blast: "Stop with the nagging, enough already. I'm on vacation. Don't I deserve a little peace and quiet?"

Unlike the times at home on my bedroom floor, when I strained to catch their conversations, this evening in the country I put my hands over my ears. I cried softly to myself, hoping my bunkmates didn't hear my parents or me. I wanted my mother and father to drop their weapons and halt their attacks. I wanted their war to be over, just like the big ones in Europe and Japan. I wanted my mother and father to hold hands, to love one another like my aunts and their husbands. I was old enough to know that happy endings were guaranteed only in fairy tales and Hollywood movies. But that night, with the country sky exploding with stars, I recited, "Star light, star bright, grant me the wish I wish tonight, A Paradise of Peace and Quiet—here in Union Pier, back home on Division Street. Pretty please."

———— ✿ ————

CHAPTER FIVE

Snow Melted,
Winter Turned to Spring

On January 7, 1946, in the early hours of a Chicago morning, a six-year-old girl on the northwest side of the city was the victim of a horrific crime. When it happened, I was only one year older than that little girl and was so traumatized by the case that I never forgot her name, details of the investigation, or other piercing events of that year.

Before news of the crime hit the streets and airwaves, the scene that Monday in our Division Street flat was typical for a wintry day: The temperature outside was only 10 degrees, so Mom fixed a breakfast of hot Malt-O-Meal for me and my 10-year-old brother, Ronnie. After insisting on adding leggings to my school outfit of corduroy skirt and knitted pullover, Mom walked us downstairs, where Dad was warming up the car.

If it was snowing, raining, or the weather was at all lousy, Dad would pack as many neighborhood kids that could fit into his four-door Buick, and deliver or fetch us from school—four long city blocks away. This day, when a patrol boy spotted a half dozen of us—bundled in fat coats, knitted caps, and neon mittens—spilling from the Buick, he nudged a kid nearby and exclaimed, "Look—it's just like the clown car at Ringling Brothers!"

After spending an uneventful day in second grade, I exited the school's double doors at 3:15 and was delighted to find Dad and his Buick waiting at the curb. My father drove the same herd back home and parked in front of our store. He sent the kids to their appreciative parents, Ronnie to Deborah Boys Club, then took my mittened hand in his to enter the store.

I was on my way to my mother to get my after-school kiss when something in the *Chicago Daily News* caught my eye. "You don't need to read that," my mother said when she saw me halt at the newspaper that was spread open on her counter. I was staring at a page in the afternoon *Red Streak* that displayed a picture of a little girl. The headline read: **Kidnap Girl 6 From Bed Here**. The story under the black-and-white photograph said that six-year-old Suzanne Degnan was asleep in the first-floor bedroom of her parents' apartment on North Kenmore Avenue, when through a window left open a few inches, someone climbed into the bedroom, kidnapped the little girl, and left a ransom note demanding $20,000 for her safe return. As I studied the girl's photo and absorbed the report, my heart was beating so loud, I was sure customers in our store could hear the thumping.

"Climbed into the bedroom," I repeated to myself. *I* slept close to the window—just like the little girl in the story. Maybe I should switch sides with Ronnie, who slept closer to the door. Back then, I never thought twice about a boy and girl sharing the same bed. In fact, I felt safer with my brother's solid shape nearby. Anyway, other families in our cramped, immigrant neighborhood had similar arrangements: Kids would get the one bedroom, while adults took the Murphy bed or a couch that opened for two. This worked well for my family, because once my parents tucked us in, they were free to stay up late, listen to the radio, and quarrel.

The girl in the newspaper photo—who slept all alone in her bedroom without a big brother at her side—had a cute round face, something like mine, and she was smiling.

She was wearing a dress with a Peter Pan collar, like the one Mother bought for me at Mandel Brothers. Under the girl's snapshot was this description: "Hair-Reddish blond, bobbed. Eyes-Blue. Weight-74 pounds and plump. Height-52 inches. Clothing at time of abduction-blue pajamas. Disposition-Cheerful and fearless."

As my trembling fingers held the newspaper, I studied the little girl's picture and wondered how my parents would describe me if I were the one snatched from my side of the bed near the window. They'd say, "Black wavy hair, green eyes, 40 pounds, 40 inches [that's what the doctor measured at my last visit], pink pajamas." That part was easy. But certainly not "cheerful and fearless." "Good little girl and a scaredy-cat" was more like it.

"*Vez meir,* the poor parents," Mrs. Schwartz said, as she craned over my shoulder to read the print, and at the same time place a package of Rinso soap powder, a bottle of Fleecy White bleach, and a carton of Lucky Strike cigarettes on Mom's counter. In a fur hat that was balding in spots, a man's long coat, and galoshes, Mrs. Schwartz looked like a Cossack stripped of his rank.

"They'll find the little girl," my mother said, tilting her head in my direction and shaking it side-to-side to prevent Mrs. Schwartz from going any further. "Once the kidnapper gets the *gelt,* he'll let her go."

As Mom added the column of grocery prices she had penciled on a brown paper bag, Mrs. Schwartz interrupted her: "Put it in the book, *bubbalah,* okay? I forgot to bring my purse." She spread her two palms before my mother, showing them empty, as if she was a thief proving her innocence.

I watched my mother's face dim as she removed her ledger book from the shelf where it was hidden.

Uh-oh, another credit customer, I thought—that's bad for business. I moved behind the counter to put my arms around my mother's waist, comforting her and myself at the same time. "Are you sure he'll let her go, Mommy?" I asked, warmed in the cosmetic fragrances that masked food remnants hugging her apron. Camay soap, Halo shampoo, and Max Factor makeup battled daily against garlicky deli meats and cheeses. I was grateful the perfumes had won out.

"Of course he'll let her go," she said, as she imprinted her red lips on my forehead and combed my hair from my face with her fingers. She turned the newspaper upside down and said, "I heard on the radio that hundreds of detectives are searching all over her neighborhood. Now go in the back and do your homework. Forget about the paper." Calmed by her words, I walked towards the kitchen, but could hear Mrs. Schwartz, who had righted the paper, say, "It says they're looking in boiler rooms, alleys and hallways, and under porches. *Gevalt!*"

On my way to the kitchen I smiled a "hello" to Mrs. Friedman, who was standing at my dad's meat counter, thumping her hand on the glass. "Hurry up already, Irv," Mrs. Friedman said. "I need a pound of ground beef for dinner." A *lantsman* from the old country, Mrs. Friedman was more Americanized than the other customer. Like my mother, she was attractive, stylishly dressed in a fitted woolen coat and matching hat, and never left her apartment without makeup and high-heeled shoes.

"Hold your horses, I'll be right there," Dad said. "I had to pick up my princess from school. You want she should walk in this weather?" I stayed to watch my dad because I knew he was about to perform his magic act and didn't want to miss a step. With his thick coat still on, Dad entered the walk-in freezer, returned with a slab of beef he had grabbed from its hook, and placed it on a wooden cutting board. Then, he tossed his coat to me and rolled up his sleeves. Like a spellbound assistant at the edge of a stage, I stared as Dad wiped his hands on his apron. With his twinkling dark brown eyes and the white fabric covering his short, round body, Dad reminded me of the snowman some kids had sculpted in the schoolyard that morning. But my dad was powerful and protective. He'd never melt away at the first burst of heat.

Hugging his coat to my small body, I smelled the cigarette smoke that clung to its fibers and I flicked away ashes that fell like snowflakes onto the sawdust floor. I watched as Dad picked up a shiny cleaver and used it to chop the raw beef into chunks. With his two stubby hands, Dad scooped the pile up, then dropped it into a metal grinder. He rotated the machine's handle with one hand, and with the other, shoved the beef through the funnel until the chunks became red braids, which dripped onto the butcher paper below.

As Dad wrapped up the ground beef, completing his act, I made my way to the kitchen in the rear of our store. When I reached the radio, I turned up its volume. The dial was set to WGN, and R.F. Hurleigh was saying how worried Mr. and Mrs. Degnan, the parents of the kidnapped girl, were. Oh no, she's still missing, I thought. I sat down, still wearing my winter coat and leggings, still carrying Dad's overcoat, as I was unwilling to shed their warmth from my shivering body.

The newscaster said Suzanne's parents "were trying to raise the ransom to satisfy the abductor and regain their child safe and unharmed." Mr. Degnan spoke, too. He was crying, and said, "I'll do anything to get my child back. All we want is Suzanne back."

Where would my parents ever get $20,000 if they had to buy me back? Would my aunts and uncles chip in, my *zadie*? Often, I heard my parents bickering about money. Some weeks Daddy couldn't even pay the delivery drivers—how could he find money to rescue me?

On the radio, Mr. Hurleigh said the police believed Suzanne was taken between 1 and 2 a.m. because that's when Mr. Degnan was awakened by the sound of his neighbor's two boxer dogs barking and the voice of his daughter saying, "But I'm sleepy. I don't want to get up." Her father thought Suzanne was talking in her sleep, so he did not go to her bedroom to investigate. Suzanne's mother said she thought she heard moaning or a soft cry coming from either Suzanne's or her 10-year-old sister Elizabeth's room. She went to the hallway and listened at both bedroom doors and, when she did not hear anything, returned to her own bed.

What if my parents thought that sounds coming from my bedroom were Ronnie and me horsing around, and then ignored the noise of an intruder? My brother would surely wake if somebody climbed in through our window, wouldn't he? Even if I couldn't yell because my voice froze like it sometimes did in nightmares, Ronnie could feel the cold air. He'd save me, wouldn't he?

That night, I searched for a star in the murky winter sky and when I found one, recited my star light, star bright prayer. I asked God to keep little Suzanne alive. I prayed the kidnapper didn't tie her up, like in the movies. I prayed my mother was right, and that as soon as he got the ransom money, the kidnapper would let Suzanne go back to her worried-sick parents.

But the next morning, on January 8th, the headline read, **Kidnapped Girl Found Slain, Dismembered, Hid in Sewer**. As I read the story under the headline, I felt as if I was going to throw up: "The head, torso, and legs were found in four different catch basins near her home. Early this morning, only the arms of the victim were missing."

"No, no!" I cried, tears falling from my eyes to the newspaper. My parents both left their work counters and ran towards me, each blaming the other for leaving the paper where I could find it. "Sshh, sshh," my mother said, wiping tears from her eyes as she hugged and tried to soothe me. "The police will find the terrible man who did this."

"Poor Suzanne, poor Suzanne," I kept saying, as I buried my face in her apron. This time, with the grisly details of the murder imprinted in my brain—as vivid as the lipstick stain my mother had planted on my forehead the day before—my mother's words and warmth could not console me. I continued to sob. Some tears were for that cheerful and fearless little girl with reddish-blonde, bobbed hair, and others for me, the dark-haired child who slept close to the window that opened onto frigid, night-marish Division Street.

"Is it closed tight?" I asked my father that evening.

"The window is locked," he said, and proved it by trying and failing to pull up the sealed window frame. "See? You have nothing to worry about."

"Can you leave the bedroom door open all the way?"

"Change places," Ronnie said. "I'll sleep near the window." In size and shape, with black hair and a boyishly handsome face, and wearing long pajamas, my brother resembled Robin in the Saturday serials we watched at the Vision Theater. But to me, his chivalry that night turned him into the bigger, braver Batman. I'm not certain why Ronnie wasn't as shattered by the crime as I was. Perhaps because he was a boy, four years older than the victim, and more daring than I, he couldn't imagine something like that happening to him.

It was easy to switch places and surrender my Division Street scene and my nightly search for stars, for I figured no one was in heaven listening to my prayers. Now, with my big brother between me and a possible ladder, with light from the kitchen and the voices of my parents drifting into our bedroom, I tried to erase thoughts of poor Suzanne.

In school the next day, one of the girls raised her hand to ask the teacher about the newspaper story. Miss Green rose from her chair, smoothed creases from the lap of her long-sleeved dress, then leaned back against her thick oak desk with her brown-spotted hands gripping its edge. "It was a terrible, terrible thing that happened," she said, "but all of the police in the city are looking for the evil man who did this. They will find him—maybe even before you get home from school today—and put him in jail. You're all safe here and in your homes. Now, let's get on with our work." My gray-haired teacher's words were reassuring, but her troubled look was not. As Miss Green turned to the blackboard, I looked around my second-grade classroom. Because I was the shortest girl in the group, and the teacher's helper, I sat in the first row, first seat. My feet—which barely touched the floor—swung back and forth. I smelled pencils and chalk dust and studied the strips of perfect penmanship streaming along the wall above the teacher's head. The bulletin board on my right was filled with compositions on lined paper—two were mine; gold stars adorned their corners. Everything looked the same as before Christmas vacation, except the Santa Claus and snowmen drawings were gone. But the room felt different: bare, cold, and as colorless as the wintry view from the classroom's enormous windows.

The afternoon *Chicago Daily News* bore the headline, **Killer's "Butcher Tub" Found, Janitor Quizzed**. Why did they have to say "butcher"? I asked myself as I read the paper someone had stuffed in the trash. Daddy's a butcher; he'd never chop up a little girl.

The newspaper said the police were questioning a janitor about Suzanne's murder because they found "the dissection chamber" in his building: "The police were encouraged because they found bits of flesh, blood and hair in the drains of three of the four washtubs. The police then realized this was where Suzanne was hacked and sawed into five or six pieces after being strangled."

Hacked, sawed, strangled—these were not second-grade words, but I knew what they meant. It was as if a Grimms' villain had escaped from his fairy-tale page and was running loose in Chicago—wicked beyond even the authors' ghoulish imaginations. The next day's paper—which I snuck a look at when my parents weren't nearby—reported that the janitor was no longer a suspect and the police released him from custody. Suzanne's killer was still at large, maybe even looking for his next little-girl victim.

That night, long after Ronnie had fallen asleep, I lay awake and imagined Suzanne's terror. My heart was beating so loud, I was surprised it didn't wake my brother. Despite the cold night, I sweated as I envisioned the killer hacking Suzanne into pieces. I squeezed my eyes tight to erase his hand lifting a meat cleaver above his head, then slamming it down on Suzanne's 52-inch body. I scooted to the foot of the bed, slid down, and padded to the bedroom door. I could hear my father's heavy snoring. If I climbed into my parents' bed now, I'd surely wake them. They needed their sleep for work, I thought. Stop being such a baby. Go back to bed. Try being fearless for once in your life.

My parents must have been as frightened as I was, because every day the killer was at large, they'd ask, "Where are you going? Who are you going to play with? What time will you be home?" I wasn't allowed to play outside—which was fine with me—but I still was terrified at night.

One evening, I could hear the radio playing in the kitchen. Above my parents' usual squabbles, I could hear *Mr. District Attorney* about to begin. But when the announcer said, "The Case of the Three Steps to Death," I heard footsteps bolt to the radio. Then, Eddie Cantor came on.

As days passed without the killer being found, the newspapers reported that "frightened and angry parents were demanding action from the police. Mayor Kelly and Chief of Detectives Storms promised to stay on the case until little Suzanne's slayer was apprehended."

Suzanne Buried While Flowers Dance In Wind was how the *Chicago Daily Tribune* described her funeral on

January 12, 1946: "Somehow, the flowers seemed symbolic of the pretty, little, blonde-haired child who had fallen into the hands of a butchering criminal last Monday morning." My parents had given up trying to shield me from the news because that was all people were talking about anyway on Division Street. As I looked at the newspaper pictures of Suzanne's small coffin about to be lowered in the ground at All Saints Cemetery, I burst into tears. What if that was me shut in a box, buried deep in the frozen dirt of Jewish Waldheim? What if I never saw my mother, father, or Ronnie ever again?

Snow melted, winter turned to spring, and still no breakthrough in the case. Finally, on June 29, a newspaper headline read: **U.C. Sophomore Seized as Burglar; Surgeons Tools Found in Room**. Five and a half months after Suzanne Degnan's kidnapping and murder, the police matched "husky six-footer" William Heirens' fingerprints with those on the ransom note left in her bedroom and arrested Heirens for the little girl's murder. Along with two sets of surgical instruments, the police found guns and items stolen from two women whose homes had been burglarized in 1945—one woman's throat had been slashed, the other had been smashed in the head.

In Heirens' parents' home, the police found in the attic "40 pairs of women's underwear and a homemade scrapbook of Nazi leaders."

The police also linked Heirens to the murder of 33-year-old Frances Brown. After he had shot and stabbed

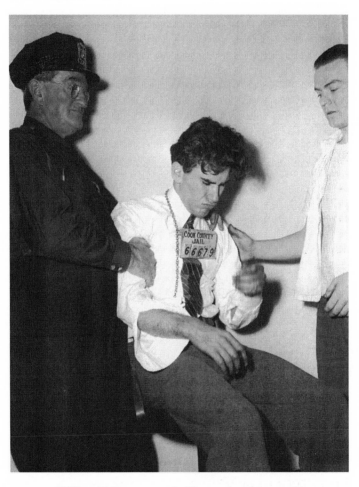

William Heirens, accused of the murder of 6-year-old
Suzanne Degnan, is photographed by police. Photo by Bill Knefel,
July 3, 1946. As published in the Chicago Sun-Times, Inc.
Copyright 2005. Chicago Sun-Times, Inc.
Reprinted with permission.

the woman, the killer took a tube of her lipstick and wrote on the wall above her bed, "For heaven's sake, catch me before I kill more. I cannot control myself." Fifty days after his arrest, and to avoid the electric chair, Heirens confessed to three murders, including Suzanne's. He was sentenced to three consecutive life terms. The next day's paper read, "Walking the streets at night is now a bit safer, now that the werewolf is in chains."

With William Heirens locked in jail for the rest of his life, I slowly regained faith in my Division Street world. School was out for the summer, and during daytimes I played outdoors, feeling carefree and sheltered once more. Little by little, I pushed away—but never completely forgot—the terrifying scenes that had haunted me for more than half a year. At bedtime, I switched sides with Ronnie and returned to the window—viewing my nighttime stage on the street below—and reciting my star light, star bright prayer. I reasoned that although God was not able to bring Suzanne back home alive, He did put her killer in jail, where he could no longer threaten little girls.

One month later, in July, my family had our own minor and amusing crime story. Dad awoke one morning to find a large steel safe wedged in his Buick's back seat. He called the police, and Ronnie and I joined our father to await their arrival. One of the cops stared at the safe in the car, slapped the side of his head, and said, "If that don't beat everything!"

Fingerprints on the safe matched those found on the back door of a nearby warehouse, and the police soon apprehended the culprits. The thieves confessed not only to robbing the warehouse, but also to "borrowing our car" at least three times previously for other burglaries. After each escapade, they returned the car to the spot where Dad had parked it the night before. This time, with the warehouse job, the *shlemiels* lacked the combination or proper tools to open it, so they lifted the safe out of the warehouse and stuffed it—like the gang of children transported to Lafayette—in Dad's sedan. For some reason, perhaps approaching footsteps, or maybe it was easier going in than out, the thieves left their booty in the Buick, where Dad had found it.

One weekday that same month, I was playing in front of our store with my friend Gloria when my father came outside. "Princess," he called to me, using one hand to shield his eyes from the sun and the other to grasp the neck of a seltzer bottle. "Can you make a delivery for me? Ronnie's at Deborah, and the customer needs it right away." With his hand aloft, and the sun bouncing off the bottle, my grinning dad looked triumphant, as if he were a prizewinner flaunting his trophy.

I dropped the yellow chalk I was using to draw hopscotch squares and ran to my dad. "Sure," I said, pleased to be considered big enough for the task. Maybe I'd even get a tip. "Who's it for?"

"Vic, Margie's husband. He's home from work with a bad stomach and phoned to ask if someone could bring up a bottle of seltzer. He thinks it will help settle his gut."

I didn't know Vic, but I liked Margie a lot. A dark-haired, shapely *shikseh,* about the age of my young uncles' girlfriends, Margie was lively and friendly. "They live on Campbell, right?" I asked.

I had often walked Margie to her apartment building, holding a small bag of her groceries for her while she dug out her keys. "Thanks, sweetheart," she would say at the entryway. "I can take it from here."

"Second floor, right," Dad said, presenting the seltzer to me.

I took the bottle from his hand, kissed his sweaty cheek, and walked around the corner to Margie's building. "Are ya coming back?" my girlfriend Gloria called out. Blonde, blue-eyed, and curly-haired, my friend—although Jewish, too—looked different from my dark-haired playmates. With her pink summer blouse and shorts, and kneeling to finish the hopscotch squares, Gloria looked like a fairy-tale sprite. Other neighborhood kids were roller-skating, riding bikes, or jumping rope. It was great to see our street back to life: children playing freely, not afraid of the bogeyman, or kidnappers.

"I'm making a delivery," I said to her, holding up the seltzer bottle, and acting like my big-shot brother rather than the half-pint I really was. "I'll be down in a minute."

I climbed the stairs to Margie's second-floor apartment and knocked on the door. "Who's there?" a man asked. "Delivery," I sang cheerfully, as if I was bringing a surprise bouquet of roses. "Special delivery from Irv's Finer Foods."

"Well, look who's here," the man—who must've been Vic—said as he opened the door. "They sent me a sweet little girl to help settle my stomach." Vic was young like

Margie, with dark eyes, chiseled cheekbones, and a thin face that ended in a pointed chin. I was relieved to see he was wearing a shirt and pair of slacks, rather than the pajamas and robe of a sick person, for that bedroom outfit would have embarrassed me. As Vic stood at the door, his eyes moved slowly from the top of my black curly hair, down my 40-inch body, all the way to my ankle socks and lace-up shoes.

Before I had a chance to ask why he was looking at me as if he was the wolf and I was Red Riding Hood, Vic took the bottle from my hand and said, "Come on in, come in, let me get some money."

As I stepped inside the apartment, I looked past him to get a peek at Margie's place. Because she wasn't Jewish, I wondered if Margie decorated her home differently than ours. I glanced around and spotted a Formica kitchen table and an ordinary enamel stove and icebox, and craned my neck to see into the living room—to perhaps find a cross with a bloody Jesus stretched along a "T." I heard Vic close the front door and turn the lock. "Can't be too careful," he said when I swiveled at the click of the deadbolt. "Say, as long as you're here, sweetheart, want to play a little game?"

"I have to get back downstairs," I said, stepping away from him. "My friend is waiting for me."

"It's a quick game. All you have to do is lie down on the floor." He took my wrist and drew me towards the bathroom. I tried to pull away, and when I felt his fingers tighten like a handcuff, my heart started to beat fast—like it did in January with all of the newspaper stories about

Suzanne Degnan. Although it was warm that day in Vic's apartment, I felt goose bumps on my arms, as if an open window let in an arctic blast, rather than a hot summer breeze.

I lay down on the floor because I was afraid, afraid he might hurt me if I didn't listen to him, afraid he would never let me out of the barricaded apartment, afraid I would never see my parents again. I thought about Suzanne—maybe if she had obeyed the kidnapper, he wouldn't have killed her and chopped her up. The black-and-white, ceramic-tiled floor where Vic told me to lie down was cold.

I closed my eyes so I couldn't see his bony hands move along my body, over and under my clothes, touching me where I knew he wasn't supposed to. When I started to cry, he stopped and said, "Okay, okay, I thought you'd like this game."

"Please, please let me go home," I said, as I stood up and smoothed my skirt.

"Of course, honey, I'm not keeping you here. It's only a game. A secret game, just between you and me. Promise not to tell anybody about it, especially your dad. Okay?"

"I promise," I said, wiping tears from my face with the back of my hand.

"Here's a nickel," he said, pressing the coin into my palm. "A tip for the special delivery."

I closed my fist on the nickel, but knew I would throw it away the minute I got downstairs. As Vic unlocked the door, he squeezed two fingers of his right hand together and drew them across his lips, as if he were zippering them shut. "Remember, our secret. You don't want your dad mad at you for playing this game, do you?"

When I got downstairs, I tossed the nickel into the street and walked back towards the store. "Are ya playing?" Gloria called to me. "Not now," I said.

"Everything go okay, Princess?" Dad asked when I strode past him, my head lowered. I nodded "yes" and Dad returned to his customer.

I didn't tell my father, or my mother, or my brother, what happened that day in Vic's apartment. I kept the secret to myself—not because Vic told me to, but because I felt too ashamed, and too stupid. I had spent all those months worrying about a faceless criminal climbing into my bedroom window, and here my very own father sent me up to Vic. I had thought my father was strong and protective, but that was a figment after all—like the snowman in the schoolyard who melted on the first warm day.

I hated my father then, almost as much as I hated Vic. And I hated myself for being such a dumb and helpless little girl. And, I knew what would happen if I told my parents. They'd call the police, like the time when I was five and a man tricked me by showing me something ugly, instead of the dolly he had promised. I'd have to describe what had happened on Vic's cold bathroom floor. Vic might be sent to jail and Margie would be left alone. Maybe she'd be mad at me for telling on him. Maybe she wouldn't believe me. Soon enough, the whole neighborhood would find out about it. People would shake their heads and whisper behind my back and feel sorry for me. My picture might even be in the newspaper, like little Suzanne Degnan's, where everyone could read about me and my shame. No, it was too horrible to think about—worse than what happened on the cold floor. I would never tell anyone. Never.

—⟋•⟍—

CHAPTER SIX

From Your Lips to God's Ears

I was standing on top of our Formica kitchen table, mod-eling a new woolen skirt Mother was shortening when she handed me a piece of jungle green cotton thread and said, "Chew this."

I stooped down to accept the two inches of wispy fiber from her fingers, thus obeying a familiar *bobemayse* (old wives' tale). This one, brought with from the Russian *shtetl* of her childhood, warned that evil spirits lurked near the pincushion, measuring tape, and scissors. If I did not chew the thread, I would be unprotected, and the demons could use the silver straight pins to stab my tender skin.

I was nine years old that weekday morning in the fall of 1947, and understood that this ritual, which accompanied the shortening of all of my clothing, was just peasant folklore. But I played along because it was a chance to be close to my mother. Although I often felt wounded by her constant supervision of my appearance—trying to get me to comb my hair, stand up straight, and eat less—I still adored her. So I'd take every chance offered, even if it meant chewing thread and swallowing superstition, to prove my fidelity and win her love.

I can't remember why I was home that morning, perhaps a head cold or school holiday, but I'm certain it was a weekday because of what happened later during the tailoring.

As Mother worked her way around the hem, folding up three inches of fabric and stabbing pins into its bulk, I asked, "How long will this take?" My words were garbled, with the wet thread getting tangled in my tongue.

"Sssh. Chew."

As I chewed, I thought about Mom's Saturday shopping trip downtown with her three sisters that produced this skirt. "Bring me back a surprise," I had pleaded as she prepared for her outing. I was thinking: book, fountain pen, or lamb's wool sweater (cashmere was out of the question), but kept mum because I didn't want to spoil the intrigue.

"Sure," she had replied, and rushed to join Mollie, Etta, and Rose. Temporarily freed of the apron she wore in our store, my mother had dressed up for the trip. With her black hair pulled back in a bun, her wide-shouldered rayon dress, and her high-heeled shoes, my mother looked as glamorous as the women in the ads of the department stores she'd be visiting. As she walked out the door, the scent of My Sin perfume trailing behind her, I wondered if I'd ever be as head-turning as she when I grew up.

Based on her daily demands of me, I think my mother was haunted by the same question: Would I favor my dad's side of the family—who were short, tubby, with their heads in the clouds? Or would I grow up to be like her side—who were slim, ambitious, and fashionable? But what my 34-year-old mother deemed fashionable in 1947, I found ugly, like the green woolen skirt I was modeling this weekday.

I remembered my excitement on the Saturday Mother had returned with the skirt. Racing to the door to relieve her of her Carson's, Stevens', and Fair's shopping bags, I shouted, "Let me see, let me see!" I tossed out the tissue paper, seeking something delightful, but instead fished out the homely, scratchy skirt.

"Isn't it pretty?" Mother had said excitedly. "I got it on sale. Try it on."

"Yes, Mom, pretty," I had said, my voice a bass to her soprano. "But I'll try it on later. Okay?" I considered telling her the truth then and there, but kept my mouth shut.

What I wanted to say was that I not only hated the green skirt, I loathed all of the clothing she bought for me. I wanted to tell her that pleated skirts made me look fat, that none of my pals wore black pullovers with red satin roses stitched above the heart, and that the one-inch wedge on my slip-on leather shoes wouldn't stop me from being the shortest child in the fourth grade. But I feared honesty might hurt her feelings or turn her against me, so I had feigned delight.

My reverie about the skirt ended at 11:30, when from my spot atop the kitchen table, I heard the hum of a familiar tune, and a deep radio voice saying, "And now, *The Romance of Helen Trent*." My mother paused at the sound of the announcer's words, straightened up and squared her shoulders, removed a straight pin she held between her red lips, and joined the speaker. Together they intoned, "The real-life drama of Helen Trent, who, when life mocks her, breaks her hopes, dashes her against the rocks of despair, fights back bravely, successfully, to prove what so many women long to prove in their own lives—that because a woman is thirty-five or more, romance in life need not be over, that romance can begin at thirty-five."

That morning, as I watched my mother recite the soap opera's opening, I thought of her as a typical listener who was caught up in the 15-minute daily dramas. It wasn't until years later, when my aunt Rose told me of my parents' courtship, that I understood what Helen Trent's romances must have meant to my mother.

"Your dad was a neighbor in our Haddon Avenue apartment building, and when he saw your mom, he fell like a ton of bricks," Aunt Rose had said after I'd pumped her for details. "Irv eventually proposed. After all, he was 24 and ready to be married, but Min was only 19 at the time. What can I tell you? Min turned him down, and told our mother that she didn't love him and would wait for romance.

"'Romance, schamance,' our mother said. 'Irv loves you and will make a good living for you. You'll learn to love him.' So with the Depression going on, and all eight of us kids still living in the house, Min took our mother's advice. Irv was ecstatic, but I don't think Min ever felt the same way."

That explains a lot, I thought, after hearing Aunt Rose's

version. But in 1947, when my mother turned wistful as she listened to the soap opera, I thought she was merely sympathetic to Helen Trent's travails. I didn't realize my mother had been pushed into an unwanted marriage, and was likely still longing for the same romance as the radio's heroine.

"Turn," Mother commanded, stepping back from the kitchen table to view the skirt's new length. As she studied me, she put her hands in the rickrack-trimmed pockets of her Swirl housecoat, and looked to me as if she were the fashion designer Elsa Schiaparelli.

I complied, raising my arms to my sides, imagining myself a long-legged model, not a shrimp who needed every article of clothing shortened. I circled the tabletop in my bobby socks, one foot in front of the other and felt the straight pins taunting my skin. But the masticated thread had done its job—there was no blood.

"Perfect. Take it off."

Mother reached up to grab my hand and help me land on the cushion of a gray padded chair that matched the pattern of our silver-rimmed Formica table.

With the hideous skirt in Mother's clutches, I put on the pajamas I was wearing before the swap and settled on the couch to finish *Black Beauty*, the hardcover book I had recently borrowed from the library. I was anxious to learn the stallion's fate as he served both cruel and gentle masters.

When *The Romance of Helen Trent* ended, Mother spun

the radio dial and it landed on a station that was playing Arthur Godfrey's version of "Too Fat Polka." As soon as I heard the popular tune, I joined Godfrey on the lyrics.

As I was about to repeat the last line, Mother rushed to the radio and switched it off.

"*Feh,* what kind of song is that?" Mother said.

"It's only a joke, Mom, a funny song." I looked down at my body, its shape concealed by worn and stretched pajamas. I pulled up my pajama top, pinched an inch of skin at my waist, and asked, "Do you think I'm too fat?"

"Now you're not," she said, as she rose from her chair. "But keep eating like your father . . ." She didn't finish the sentence. We both knew its familiar ending. Instead, she moved to the Singer Blackside sewing machine that stood in the corner of our kitchen. The Singer's coal-black chassis reminded me of Black Beauty, for it was shaped like the head and torso of the young horse. Although Mother was keeping me company in the house that weekday morning, she wore lipstick, rouge, and mascara—as if her cherished Singer deserved the courtesy. I often had the same thought: that the regal machine merited more than our humble kitchen.

With my book still unopened on my lap, I studied my mother. Once seated at her Singer, she rested her wedge-heeled house slippers on the black-grated treadle. I had to turn away from the sight of her feet, because her swollen toes always disturbed me. Daily, my mother jammed her feet into narrow bargain basement high heels and her big toes retaliated by sprouting painful bunions.

*This is what Mom's Singer sewing machine looked like
as it stood in the corner of our kitchen.*

I watched instead as she took the spool of thread that had earlier donated my snack, and deposited it on a bobbin that would dance to the motor's music. As she flattened her house slippers on the grill, Mother used the fingers of both hands to push the skirt's folded hem forward. When her feet pressed the treadle up and down, a straight eye-pointed needle that had swallowed the green thread, rose and fell, magically transferring the thread from bobbin to skirt, sealing the hem's fate forever.

Daydreaming, I saw the Singer appalled at its place among white-enameled appliances, like our chipped stove and icebox. I smiled as I imagined it distastefully sniffing cooking odors that wafted to its corner and stained the kitchen walls yellow and gray. Poor Singer. On Friday nights, you must endure chicken soup simmering on the stove, emitting its therapeutic fumes of poultry, salt, carrots, and onions. If it is a Monday night, when Mom has chopped pieces of chicken skin and is frying them in *schmaltz* to make *gribbeners*—my favorite snack, I envision the Singer wincing disgustedly at the scent of sizzling grease. Secretly, I enjoyed the machine's distress, because I was jealous of its bond with my mother. I often watched the two of them—coupled with their love of sewing—and wished there was a place there for me.

Many years later, long after the Singer had been retired, and as Mother and I reminisced about her old companion, I asked why she had never taught me to sew. Brushing the dust from a needlepoint portrait she had recently completed and hung on the wall, Mother answered, "You never asked. Your nose was always in a book, like your father's. I never thought you were interested."

She was right about one thing: I *was* like my dad, who stashed Mickey Spillane or other paperbacks near his meat counter.

But I think another reason Mom never taught me to sew, or to knit, or do needlepoint, was that she was gifted at these crafts, and wanted to keep this talent for herself. Perhaps after giving up her girlish dreams of romance, she refused to relinquish one more part of herself.

Along with my jealousy of the Singer, I resented the machine because it was a haughty reminder of my height handicap. Evidently my mother sensed my distress, because two weeks after the skirt shortening, when my parents thought I was asleep in my bedroom, I overheard this kitchen conversation:

"I think we should take her to see someone." It was my mother talking.

"You're nuts," Dad said.

"She's the smallest girl in her class," Mother said. "Maybe there's something wrong that a doctor can fix." From your lips to God's ears, I thought, repeating an expression I had often heard my mother say.

"There's nothing wrong with her. She's perfect the way she is," Dad said. His rebuttal didn't surprise me, for we were a family of shorties: Neither he nor my mother reached 5'5"; my 12-year-old brother Ronnie was short for his age; and I—my father's princess—was the runt of the litter.

I lifted myself on my elbows the better to hear the rest of their conversation. Surprisingly, I was rooting for Mother. If a doctor could fix me up, give me a pill to make me taller, like the rest of my classmates, maybe then people would stop patting me on the head as if I was a pet. Whenever I saw a palm headed for my crown, I'd duck and steer the hand away. I wanted so much to be normal size, not this midget who gets lost in a crowd. Not this baby who has to sit on the Yellow Pages to reach the kitchen table. Not this dwarf perched at a classroom desk, feet never touching the floor.

I fell asleep before I knew who won the evening's skirmish, but by morning I learned Mom was victorious. Yea! I thought to myself, the doctor will give me some magic pills and I will grow tall, slim, and beautiful.

The day before our appointment with the doctor,

Mother said to me, "I think we should do something with your hair. It could use some body." She was holding a box of Toni Home Permanent, and her blue eyes glistened, like those of a mad scientist. Maybe Mother had read my mind and believed that hair waves—like Elizabeth Taylor's in *National Velvet*—would take care of the "beautiful" part of my goal, and the doctor would handle the "tall" part. I had heard the frequent "Which Twin has the Toni?" radio commercials and marveled how the simple $2 treatment could be achieved at home, rather than at a beauty parlor where a professional wave could cost $15. As I pondered Mother's proposal, I walked to the bathroom, stood on tiptoes to see into the mirror, and used the fingers of both hands to fluff up my hair.

I returned to the kitchen, still not certain I wanted to be part of an experiment, but Mother had already assumed my compliance. Preparing her laboratory, she laid out a Pyrex mixing bowl, a pair of cruddy towels, rubber gloves, and the ingredients contained in the Toni kit.

"Sit," she ordered, and placed the larger of the blighted towels around my shoulders.

"It smells terrible," I said, coughing and pulling the towel up to cover my nose.

"Don't breathe," Mother suggested, as she steadily rolled strands of my hair on plastic curlers, clasped them shut with their elastic bands, then brushed the magic potion on each completed curl.

"Ouch," I complained when she tightened the rolls.

"It hurts to be beautiful," she said.

As I touched my throbbing scalp, I wondered if a snip

*An advertisement for Toni Home
Permanent that likely convinced
my mother I was a candidate
for the popular product.*

of thread or other Yiddish charm could dull the pain, but declined to ask. Instead, I pointed to the wedding portrait that hung in our entry hall above the telephone table and said, "You don't look like you're in pain in that picture." Mother paused to follow my gaze, but did not respond. She returned to my hair, the curlers, and the lotion—her silence lingering in the air like the Toni's strong fumes.

Every time I passed the tinted photograph, I'd pause to admire the couple captured in 1933. My mother looked angelic in a floor-length white dress with a train that pooled at her feet. She held an enormous bouquet of roses, almost too wide for her tiny figure. Her veil was simple, with lilies of the valley tucked at each ear. My dad looked debonair in his tuxedo, white shirt, white bow tie, and a sprig of lilies of the valley decorating his lapel. The backdrop hinted that the young couple were being photographed at a fancy hotel or banquet hall. But it was an illusion: My parents were posed before the portrait studio's painted scenery. I often wondered as I studied that photo, how my parents must have felt when they had to remove their lavish wedding costumes, return them to the photographer's wardrobe rack, then slip into their Depression-era marriage.

On Saturday morning as Mother and I were dressing for our trip downtown to see the doctor, I stared at my image in the bathroom mirror and said, "I look like Orphan Annie." I tried to push my fingers through the new ringlets and thought to myself, Elizabeth Taylor—who do you think you're kidding?

The wedding portrait that hung in our entry hall.
My parents look marvelous, but the clothing, flowers,
and backdrops were props.

"I probably wound the rollers too tight," Mother admitted. "In a few days, the curls will loosen up and you'll be gorgeous."

"From your lips to God's ears," I said, making my mother laugh.

As we waited on the corner of Division and Campbell for a streetcar that would take us downtown to see the Big Man in His Field, an endocrinologist, I asked my mother, "Can I sit by the window?"

"Sure, who needs to see outside anyway?" she answered, and we stepped aboard the red Pullman that stopped on tracks a few steps from the sidewalk. We were both wearing lightweight fall coats that day, "like Toni Twins," my mother had said when we fastened our buttons in front of the hall mirror. Her coat had padded shoulders and a hemline that swung gracefully at three-quarter length. My coat, the same navy blue color, stopped at my knees—a length preferable to its original hem that had tickled my ankles.

Once on board the streetcar, Mother took a quarter from her purse and handed it to the conductor, who made change for the 10-cent fare with the coin holder he wore on his belt. Then, with the car in motion, we lurched through the aisle until we found two empty spaces. After we landed on the cane-backed seats, I tugged at Mother's coat sleeve and said, "Look, there's Mrs. Schwartz, she's going into the A&P."

Mother turned to stare past me out the streetcar window towards the supermarket that had recently opened across from our grocery store. "Eggs, forty-nine cents a dozen," she read from a sign posted on the A&P's giant windows. "Chickens, forty-two cents a pound," she continued, slowly shaking her head from side to side. Her padded shoulders sagged and she looked on the verge of tears as she turned her eyes from the window and focused on the coins the conductor had given her. I watched her open her pocketbook, fish out a small purse, and drop the coins in. After clicking it closed, she pulled the handbag towards her chest, lowered her head, and said—in a voice I could barely hear—"We can't even buy eggs for forty-nine cents. How can we fight them?"

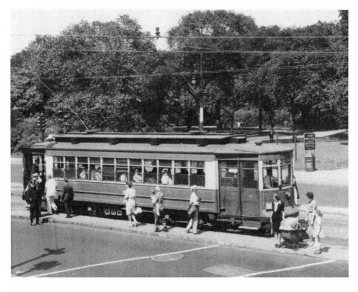

The type of red Pullman streetcar that Mother and I took
for our downtown appointment. Courtesy of the
Chicago Transit Authority.

"Why was Mrs. Schwartz going to the A&P?" I asked. "I thought she was our customer."

"When she has to charge, she's our customer," Mother said, her voice as serious as the announcer on *Helen Trent*. I didn't pursue the subject further, for I knew the store's traffic was a sore point, so we sat silently as the A&P shrunk, then disappeared from view.

As the Pullman moved along its route, I scanned Division Street and looked for other changes to my neighborhood. I felt a pang when we passed the empty space that once was the stable. Before it closed up and moved away, my friends and I would gather outside its wide open doors and watch Mr. Smolinski care for the horses. Peddlers, like my uncle Jack or my *zadie,* would bring their animals to the stable for grooming and feeding. Despite the reek of manure and stale hay, my pals and I would watch Mr. Smolinski pound a U-shaped metal plate to the horse's hoof, or force a bronze slice into its mouth. Brownie was my favorite beast, and I'd pretend he was young and swift, instead of the tired and scabbed nag he really was. I saw myself in stirrups atop a saddle, as if I were the movie star cowgirl Dale Evans, and could almost hear Brownie whinny as we galloped into the sunset. But the stable and horses were gone now. Most of the peddlers had moved on, and those that remained roamed our alleys in clunky trucks, instead of quaint horse-drawn wagons.

The doctor's office was on Wabash Avenue in a building that looked out on the El tracks. After riding an elevator to its floor, Mother gave my name to a pert blonde sitting behind a glass partition, then we took seats in the waiting room. Before opening *The Saturday Evening Post* that I had removed from a cluttered table between the two of us, I gazed at my mother, who was filling out a form the blonde had given her. She was wearing plastic Shasta daisies clipped to her small ears and her shirtwaist dress was sky-blue like her eyes and eye shadow.

Envious of the height her high-heeled shoes had won her, I rose from my chair, placed my magazine down to save my seat, and strolled to a mirror that hung near the coat rack.

Standing on tiptoes, I steadied myself with my right hand on the back of a chair, then lifted my left above my Orphan Annie head. In the illusion, I saw myself stretched to average height. Just average, I thought. No higher, just average. I suspected Mother concurred and believed that if I was taller, I would have better luck in life than her—that I'd find romance, like the radio's Helen Trent. Maybe Mother thought a handful of inches might win me a doctor or lawyer, and spare me a butcher and an apartment above a store.

A heavy-set woman in a flowered dress came through a door that led from the examining rooms to the waiting area. She was waving a thick arm to someone behind her. "Thank you, Doctor," she said. I watched as her arm's flesh flapped back and forth, like bedsheets drying on a clothesline. She wore a grin on her round face, and I fancied the doctor had just announced, "It's your glands." Relieved of her guilt, the bulky woman retrieved her circus-tent coat and left the office happily. What if that was me as a grown up? Short *and* fat, like my dad's two sisters. No wonder

Mother dragged me to the doctor. She was probably trying to shield me from the slings I had been silently sending the heavyweight patient.

A nurse with a white cap atop her long brown hair followed behind the woman. She was wearing a white uniform and white shoes, and clasped a clipboard to her chest. "The doctor will see you now," she said, and opened the door wide to indicate the path. Mother took my hand, nervously squeezing my fingers, as if she was the one learning her fate, and not her nine-year-old daughter.

In the examining room, the nurse pointed Mother to a chair and me to a padded table. "Hop up," she said. As I used a step stool to climb aboard, I scanned the room and squinted at the diplomas that lined the walls. Calligraphy and gold seals confirmed the medicine man's standing, and I was encouraged at his power to mold my future. The nurse recorded my blood pressure on the chart, then led me to a scale. As she lowered the bar to gauge my height, and moved a balance to find my weight, I felt as if I was Black Beauty being judged for sale.

I returned to my place on the cushioned table and stared at a chart that was hung on the wall opposite the doctor's diplomas. Drawings of children, lined up like Russian nesting dolls, hopped across the poster.

When the doctor entered the room, I noticed his antiseptic smell, his intimidating height, gray hair, and his short white coat. His name was stitched above the pocket, but the years have erased it from my memory. "Let's take a look," he said, closing the door behind him. He studied the clipboard the nurse had handed him, then without looking up, spoke to my mother in a slow voice, as if she were the fourth grader and not I. "Well," he said, "she is shorter than her age group, but her weight is just right. According to the intake sheet you filled out, I see that you, your husband, and your son are short people. It's unlikely your daughter will grow much taller than either one of you. I don't recommend hormone injections at this time."

"Thank you, Doctor," Mother said, her voice sounding as glum as when we were on the streetcar and she was reading the A&P prices. Then my mother recovered, smiled at the doctor like a shy fan, and said, "We just wanted to make sure."

As I stepped off the examining table, I felt a mixture of disappointment and relief. I was short—like my parents and brother—but not a midget, nor a dwarf, nor a freak. And the doctor said my weight was just right.

Mother turned to me, took my face in her two hands, kissed my forehead, and said to me loud enough for the departing physician to hear, "I knew you were perfect just the way you were."

I was happy to get her kiss and hear her sugary words. But in my heart, the one beating beneath red satin roses, I knew Mother's efforts to transform her only daughter were far from over—just temporarily stalled.

———◦∿◦———

CHAPTER SEVEN

Searching for the Spotlight

I n 1948, the tiny country of Israel gained statehood, President Truman defeated Governor Dewey, and my brother Ronnie became a man. While the first occasion was significant for Zionists, and the second for Democrats, it was the latter event—Ronnie's bar mitzvah—that was the year's highlight for the Shapiro family of Division Street.

Several months before my brother's rite of passage—which was scheduled for May 22, less than a week after his 13th birthday—my grandfather visited us in our grocery store to discuss the ceremony, and a celebration. "Just the *shul*, Pa," I heard my mother say to her father as they gabbed near the cash register. "Ronnie will read from the Torah, we'll have a kiddush with wine and sweets in the synagogue, and that'll be it. We can't lay out money for a hotel party."

"*Meshuggana*," *Zadie* said, leaning across Mom's counter to shake her bony shoulder. "My first grandchild born in this country and we don't have a *simcha* [celebration]? What will people think—we're too cheap to throw a party?"

This Government has been informed that a Jewish state has been proclaimed in Palestine, and recognition has been requested by the *provisional* Government thereof.

The United States recognizes the provisional government as the de facto authority of the new Jewish *State of* ~~state~~. Israel.

Harry Truman

Approved,
May 14, 1948.

6.11

A copy of the May 14, 1948, document signed by President Harry S. Truman recognizing the Jewish state of Israel.

Wearing a well-worn shirt rolled up at the cuffs, and brown slacks stained by the wooden crates of ice-packed fish he schlepped into his store, my grandfather didn't look like someone crazy for a fancy-dress fete.

"Let's have a party," I said, echoing my grandfather.

I was standing at my mother's elbow, wearing my store apron over a plain blouse and skirt, but I quickly envisioned myself dressed in fancy party clothes and dancing to the melodies of a Kay Kyser–like orchestra.

"Look, Pa, look here," Mom said, and pushed a copy of the *Chicago Daily News* in front of her father. "A&P, Jewel, National." She was flipping through the newspaper's pages, and paused to place a flat hand on several of them. "Full-page ads. How long do you think our customers will shop at our small store when they can go across the street or down the block to a supermarket where they can have aisles of stock to choose from at cheaper prices?"

My dad was at his meat counter, and both he, and the woman accepting a wrapped package from his hands, turned at Mother's sharp tone. The customer was unfamiliar, like several of the newcomers who rented the apartments being vacated by our old friends. Postwar prosperity had enabled some of our neighbors—formerly European refugees—to move up to the middle class. And this new affluence, plus more affordable automobiles, propelled them out of our inner-city neighborhood to communities farther north and south, like Albany Park and South Shore. Some people, whose incomes and aspirations climbed even higher, moved to suburbs like Skokie and Park Forest.

The newcomers were "greenhorns" who were just off the boat from Europe, plus a sprinkling of Negroes from the South and a dash of Hispanics. This lower-income population moved into our area for the same reasons as the Jews, Poles, and Italians they replaced: $25-a-month apartments, good public transportation, and the dream of jobs. But unlike our old neighbors, who were steady customers, the newcomers popped into our grocery store for a pound of ground beef or loaf of bread. And these paltry provisions discouraged neighborly chitchat.

Dad followed behind his customer to Mom's register. After the woman paid her small bill and left the store—with the bell above the door jingling her exit and echoing in the bleak space—the bar mitzvah conversation resumed.

"Maybe you should listen to your father, honey," Dad said to Mom. "A little party, maybe we can swing a little party. I heard President Truman say on the radio that good times are ahead. All those returning GIs with money to spend, all those new houses being built for them." Dad's face brightened with his words and I could easily see him swaying to the music, living it up in a good-looking suit— double-breasted, perhaps, to mask his girth.

"Please, Mommy, a party," I said, thinking such a festivity might cheer my folks, perhaps lighten the gloom brought on by the loss of old neighbors and store receipts.

Mother looked around the store that was now empty of customers, glared at my father's hopeful face and my smaller version, then shook her head. With one hand she brushed back loose hair that had escaped its nest atop her head, then pulled off a clip-on earring. She rubbed the sore spot the earring had given her and placed the plastic jewelry on the counter. Then, she moved the newspaper from *Zadie*'s line of sight and shoved it in front of Dad's. I stood on tiptoes to see, too, and watched as she turned stacks of pages. When she reached the real estate ads, she slid the newspaper back and forth between her husband and father as if she were dealing a hand of pinochle. "Vets down payment $1,000," she read aloud. She looked up at the three of us bent over the ads and pointed to black-and-white photos of houses.

"Do you think these ranch homes, New England colonials, three-, four-bedroom houses are on Division Street?" she asked. Mother's sarcastic questioning silenced me, but the men's weak stabs at a response reminded me of one of our favorite radio programs, *It Pays to Be Ignorant.* That silly quiz show was funny, though, and Mom was deeply serious.

"No," she said, "the houses are in the suburbs. You think the veterans are going to keep their families in the city with the noise and the *schmutz*? They're like everybody else—they want peace and quiet. They want better schools for their kids, garages, backyards."

Zadie took the newspaper from Mother's agitated, skinny fingers, closed its pages, and turned the paper upside down so only the sports page emerged. "I'll pay for the party," he said.

"No, Pa, no," Mother said, shaking her head. She used her thumb and its neighbor to stroke her reddened ear, then used the other hand to return the earring to its lucky place.

"Only a loan," Dad said to his father-in-law, then offered his hand, man to man, for a shake to seal the deal.

My mother looked at her father and mine, waved a hand in the air as if it were a white flag signaling surrender, and left the counter. I followed behind her and when

I caught up, put an arm around her slim waist, and said, "Don't be sad, Mommy. It'll be fun. Ronnie's party will be fun."

"Deeper and deeper," she said—more to herself than to me. She removed a balled-up Kleenex from her skirt pocket and dabbed at the mascara that had escaped her lashes.

A month before the bar mitzvah, while Ronnie was memorizing his portion and my parents were planning the party at the Somerset Hotel—with funds borrowed from *Zadie*—I decided to try my own hand at Hebrew School. The Orthodox synagogue where Ronnie would be bar mitzvahed excluded girls from the honor, but we could attend its *cheder*. Despite no chance at a Torah reading when I turned 13, let alone a party, I was envious of my brother's religious class, imagining it to be a secret club with its own language. And since English was my best subject at Lafayette Grammar School, I was certain deciphering another tongue would be a breeze.

"Are you sure you're going to stick to it?" Mother asked when I said I wanted to learn the *aleph, beth, gimels* backwards. "Even if there's no bar mitzvah?"

My mother's skepticism was justified. At nine and a half, I had already gained a reputation as a dabbler—one who leaps enthusiastically into a new activity, only to dump it at the first sign of boredom or incompetence. Half-finished oven mitts and lanyards from the Humboldt Park Fieldhouse, failed swim instruction at the Division Street YMCA, and indoor roller skates barely scuffed at the Rainbow Arena, testified to my habit.

*The Austrian-Galician Congregation at 1357 North California
Avenue, the scene of Ronnie's bar mitzvah. Today it is
a Hispanic church. Photo courtesy of Robb Packer,
copyright 2005.* Doors of Redemption: The Forgotten
Synagogues of Chicago and Other Communal Buildings.

"Yes, Mommy," I said. Not only was I keen on self-improvement, and jealous of my brother, but I also envied my Catholic classmates who floated from our public school every Wednesday afternoon with their vivid catechism cards and rosaries. I wanted a similar privilege. But true to my pattern, I lasted only two weeks at Hebrew School. Unprepared for the dark, musty schoolroom, the black-coated rabbi with his long white beard, ferocious teaching style, and disdain for little girls—as well as lessons both perplexing and boring—I quickly wanted out.

Since I flunked at *cheder*, I sought another chance to try something that might put me in the spotlight: I enrolled at Joe Keith's Dance Studio. My cousin Estherly Kaplan, one year younger than I, had already signed up for ballet. Envious of her pink tights and tutu and possible applause at a recital, I begged for lessons. But unlike my taller, thinner, shyer cousin—and because I couldn't picture myself flattened even shorter by ballet slippers, or as graceful as a swan—I opted for tap. And my mother, who was aware of my brief attention span, but perhaps sympathetic to my second-class status in the synagogue, found funds for the tuition. (Later in life, I learned that Mom had kept a secret bank account during our years on Division Street. Terrified that the store's debts would leave us penniless, she squirreled away any extra cash that reached her hands before Dad's.)

One day, as I was practicing my time step for the recital—shuffle, hop, step, flap, step—I thought about my brother's upcoming bar mitzvah. If it wasn't for my grandfather's prodding, I'm not certain Ronnie would have undertaken the rigorous year of study. My brother was not as enamored of schooling as I was, and our family attended synagogue services only one time a year—during the Jewish High Holy Days of Rosh Hashanah and Yom Kippur. Sometimes, though, I wished we were more observant, like my mother's sisters.

On the Friday evenings we visited Aunt Mollie in the sprawling apartment of the two-flat they had recently purchased in Albany Park, I'd long for my mother to stand at the head of a lace-covered dining room table like her older sister, and light candles and recite the blessings.

But at our Formica kitchen table on Division Street, we merely acknowledged the Sabbath with matzo ball soup and challah. There was no doubt we were Jewish. After all, we relished delicatessen foodstuff, sprinkled our conversations with Yiddish, denounced anti-Semitism, and applauded louder for Jewish stage and film stars, and the occasional sports figure. We supported Israel's push for statehood, but believed Israel to be a homeland for Jewish exiles, not a place for us to "make *aliyah*" or relocate to. And we did display a blue-and-white Jewish National Fund *pushke* on our kitchen counter. When coaxed, we'd drop pennies through the slot for Jewish orphans or refugees, but if short on milk money or streetcar fare, we'd retrieve the same coins from the charity box.

As I continued to shuffle, hop, step, flap, and step, I felt grateful to have my own chance at the spotlight three months after Ronnie's bar mitzvah. I smiled to myself as I recalled the first time Estherly and I rode the streetcar, on our own, to Wabash Avenue downtown for dance lessons. Dressed in outfits a step up from school clothes and carrying our dancing shoes in drawstring sacks, we had thought we were big shots. We were unaware that Estherly's mom—my aunt Etta—was following behind us in the next car. "Once I was sure you knew where to get off and how to find the building, I felt better about the two of you traveling alone," she revealed when we returned home that afternoon.

If Aunt Etta had traveled with us that first Saturday, and on the ones that followed, she might have raised her eyes at, or discouraged, the overly friendly conductor who had asked for a kiss on the cheek along with our fares. She would have smiled, though, at the shtick Estherly and I ad-libbed every time the streetcar approached the bridge over the Chicago River.

"It's going up," Estherly would cry out, as the trolley paused at the water's edge. While we'd watch the jaws of the bridge unfold and reach for the sky, and the tall sails slip below the open bridge, Estherly would add, "What if it doesn't shut back down tight? What if it falls apart when we cross it, and we plunge into the river?"

"I can't swim," I would wail, and clutch Estherly's sleeve as if I were a starlet in a B movie. "Save me!" Once the streetcar made it safely over the closed bridge, we'd laugh at our pretend terror.

My recital was still several months away, but Ronnie's big day was finally upon us. On the mild May morning of his bar mitzvah, our family walked in silence to the Austrian-Galician *shul* on California Avenue. My brother was wearing the new suit that Mom had finished shortening the night before, and I was in a stiff green dress with a Peter Pan collar and puffy short sleeves. We followed behind our parents, and I watched—hoping that this time—they might hold hands for the stroll. But Dad, in his double-breasted herringbone suit, held a cigarette in one hand, and used the other to remove bits of tobacco from his lips. Mom, outfitted in a gray silk shantung dress that shimmered with each of her high-heeled steps, kept her gloved hands tight on her pocketbook. With her black felt hat and veil (the "rooftops of Paris look"), Mother was the unquestionable beauty of the bunch.

She was also wearing the dark mink stole that Dad had

given her the Sunday before, on Mother's Day. Although his gift had initially caused a flare-up, I was happy to see that she had relented and would be entering the synagogue embraced in the soft fur.

The present that Ronnie and I had given her caused no problem, only delight as she unwrapped the blue leather jewelry box.

My brother and I had pooled our savings to swing the $3 gift and smiled proudly as she proclaimed, "It's perfect! I'll put my pearls here, my earrings here, and my broaches here." She was pointing to the box's felt compartments, and I pictured her costume jewelry, suffused with the smells of her cosmetics and perfume, nestled happily in its new home.

When Dad had placed a large silver box before her, his face was bright with excitement and likely greedy for a reaction one hundred times greater than the one granted our jewelry case. Mom opened the lid of Dad's gift, removed the white paper, and lifted out the beautiful mink stole. "Irv, you know we can't afford this," she had said, and slowly replaced the mink in its tissue nest. "We have so many bills . . ."

"I bought it on time," Dad had said, and reached deep into the silver box to retrieve the stole. "Just try it on. You'll look gorgeous in it." He held the mink stretched out between his two pudgy hands, smiling like a wholesale furrier flattering a dubious client. "You deserve a mink. And I'll pay it off. Don't worry. Just try it on."

"Please try it on," Ronnie and I had pleaded. At the time,

I was just a little girl who adored her father and couldn't bear his disappointment. I could not have appreciated my mother's struggle to keep us afloat, and saw her only as an ungrateful wife who had crushed my father as surely as a runaway truck. I remember thinking to myself, Just take it, Mom, for Daddy's sake. Just take it.

And once my mother had placed the lovely fur around her thin shoulders, and considered her stylish reflection in the bedroom mirror above the dresser—perhaps imagining herself in the spotlight like Barbara Stanwyck in *Double Indemnity*—she agreed to keep the stole and monitor Dad's monthly installments.

Once inside the synagogue, Ronnie and my dad proceeded to the men's section on the first floor and Mom and I went upstairs to join the women. After a long, tedious morning service, my brother went up to the *bimah,* then climbed atop a wooden Coca-Cola crate to reach the podium. Our grandfather stood at his side, and using his one good eye and a *yad* pointer to track the squiggly alphabet, guided Ronnie confidently through his biblical passage. As I watched my brother, radiant in his spot before the Eternal Light, his yarmulke adding authenticity to his boyish body, I gave a sidelong glance at my mother. A woman who was sitting in the row behind us placed a gloved hand on Mom's shoulder and said to her, "Such *naches,* Min, *mahzel tov.*"

Naches, pride, I thought. I could feel tears about to blur my vision, so I turned my face back to the stage, and scolded myself for my erupting envy. I loved my brother, that was for sure, and was also proud of his performance that day. But as I watched my mother's blue eyes sparkle through the veil of her hat, I wished her love for me would flow as easily as it did for him.

My mother's unconditional love for her firstborn son often confused me. I had always assumed that one of her problems with me was that I looked more like my dad than I did her. But Ronnie—although athletic in body— was short, too, and his face was the mirror image of my dad's. Why then did my brother get a pass on her obsession with weight and height?

My mother—despite possessing the brains to hold our floundering grocery business together—valued good looks and popularity over good grades and book smarts; and Ronnie bested me in both contests.

Fortunately for me, my dad leveled the playing field. Once, for a fourth-grade English assignment, I had written a poem about Ronnie. (Something about how much I adored my older brother.) After school that day, I raced into the store, flashed a sheet of composition paper before my father's eyes, and with a grin from ear to ear, said, "Look, Daddy, an E+!"

My dad brushed his hands back and forth across his butcher's apron to wipe them clean, then reached for the school assignment. As he read the poem to himself, his lips moved slightly and his brown eyes filled with tears. "Can I keep this?" he asked. When I nodded "yes," he folded the blue-lined paper several times and tucked it into his wallet. Later that day, as I was straightening up the Bayer aspirin bottles and Ipana toothpaste tubes in my sundries section of the store, I saw Dad approach Mrs. Levinson. "Rose," he said, pulling her by the elbow and thrusting the poem in front of her face. "Look what my princess wrote. See the E+."

Mrs. Levinson, and all of the other customers he waylaid that day, and for months afterwards, offered appropriate flattery to both my father and me. That composition paper—battered by his frequent unfolding, folding, and replacing—eventually weakened at its creases and the words became blurred. But the fourth-grade poem never left its home in Dad's wallet.

On the bar mitzvah morning, after his elevation, my brother's face was flushed with pride and relief when the synagogue president and rabbi rushed to his side for back-slapping, handshakes, and *mahzel tovs.* As I watched the main floor proceedings, I pondered my upcoming dance recital: Would I be as proficient as my brother in the spotlight? What if nerves overtook me on stage, and I was to stumble, trip, fall splat?

My attention drifted from my brother to my imagined future performance. If I bungled the shuffle, hop, step, flap, step, there'd be worried looks from my fellow dancers and giggles from the audience. I pictured Ronnie in his seat between Mom and Dad, his fingers over his mouth to stifle laughter. My dad would lay a threatening hand on Ronnie's shoulder and Mom would close her eyes, regretting the hard-earned money wasted on frivolous

Me, cutting a rug at Ronnie's bar mitzvah.

dance lessons. I shook away my calamitous thoughts and joined my mother as we filed downstairs to bestow hugs on my giddy brother.

In the evening party that capped Ronnie's coming of age, my dad—exhilarated from his son's morning performance and proud of the shindig he was hosting—drank more glasses of schnapps than he could handle. We had all linked arms to form a ring for the *hora* Israeli folk dance and were whirling around the floor. Several of my young uncles took turns breaking from the ring to dance the *kazatska* in the center. With arms folded across their sinewy chests, they squatted almost to the floor, shot their legs alternately out in front of them, then hopped upright with a whoop. We clapped and cheered to egg the boys on. But when my *shikker* father leapt dizzily into the spotlight, I became alarmed. Didn't the doctor tell him to watch himself? To stop smoking? To lose weight? Didn't the doctor warn Dad that his diabetes could weaken his heart as it did his feet, his gums? He had almost lost a limb to gangrene, and I had already witnessed Dad's false teeth floating nightly in a drinking glass. What other part of his body would be next to fail?

Yanking the elbow of his herringbone suit, and shouting to be heard over the orchestra's horns and relatives' hoots, I screamed, "Daddy, stop, you'll get sick!"

With his brown eyes as bright as the morning's Eternal Flame, Dad brushed my anxious hand from his sweat-soaked suit, and slurred, "I'm having a good time, Princess, let me have a good time."

Dad, tipsy, with Uncle Hy.

As for the bar mitzvah boy, throughout the evening, partygoers stuffed cash, checks, and savings bonds into the pockets of his new suit. Afterwards, when we returned home from the hotel, my parents and Ronnie went into our bedroom to count his haul. "You take it," my brother said, as he handed them a stack of money. He was leaning against the pillows, looking exhausted from being onstage from morning to night. "You can use it to pay *Zadie* back," he yawned. "I'll keep the savings bonds."

I watched from the door of the bedroom, toothpaste foaming in my mouth, as first my mother, then my father turned down Ronnie's offer. "No, no," they said—both with tears in their eyes—"it's your money, you keep it." After a few back-and-forth rounds, with tepid refusals on our parents' part, Mother said, "You're a wonderful son." She kissed him on the cheek, then crammed the money inside a dresser drawer. "A real mensch," Dad added, kissing his son's other cheek. Then, with Ronnie and me looking on, our parents hugged and kissed one another. My brother and I stared at them: This was an unfamiliar embrace! It was as if *Adonai*—mindful of Ronnie's study and sacrifice—had slipped into our Division Street bedroom, and performed a miracle right before our astonished eyes.

My parents repaid our grandfather with my brother's gifts, Ronnie abandoned his religious studies immediately after his bar mitzvah, and we all returned to the activities that had occupied us before his coming of age. For me, it was practicing for the recital. Shuffle, hop, step, flap, step, I repeated as I attempted the simple time step on the linoleum floor of our kitchen. The silver plates on my black patent leather shoes failed to make the bright pings that bounced off the wooden floor of the dance studio. But imagining myself Ann Miller in the movie *Easter Parade*, I continued to shuffle, hop, step, flap, step. I was dressed in ordinary playclothes that practice day, but pictured the costume I'd be wearing onstage. I saw the black top hat, short black tuxedo jacket, white vest with sequins, and black satin shorts. I could even envision my face, which would be completely covered in greasepaint purchased from Leo's Dancewear, that could be seen from the first rows of the Civic Theatre.

A few weeks before the recital, Aunt Etta and Estherly came to our store to meet Mom and me for our Saturday activities. The two sisters would be joining Mollie and Rose for department store browsing, and my cousin and I would be off to final rehearsals.

That's when Aunt Etta broke the news. "Maury found a place," she said. My mother remained silent. "It's a butcher shop in South Shore, and we'll be renting a beautiful six-room apartment nearby. Maury can walk to work from the building."

"Are you moving?" I asked, turning from my aunt to my cousin. To myself I thought, no more Sunday rides together in Dad's car? No more play-acting on the streetcar? No more dance lessons taken together?

As my cousin looked to her mother for an answer, my own mother found her voice. "I'm happy for you, Etta," she said, but her tone was serious like the time she challenged her father about the cost of Ronnie's party. Then, she put her arms around her younger sister and said, "Six rooms? So Estherly and David will have their own bedrooms? You'll have a dining room?"

Stepping back from her sister's embrace, and taking both of my mother's hands in hers, Aunt Etta said, "Wait and see, you'll move from Division Street one day, too. You'll get rid of the store. You'll get a bigger apartment in a better neighborhood. Be happy for me; this is good for Maury, for our family. We'll still meet downtown on Saturdays. We'll still see each other, just not every day."

Standing in the wings of the gigantic stage of the Civic Theatre on the afternoon of the recital, I peered out at the audience of family and friends. I could spot Aunt Etta, Uncle Maury, and cousin David—their faces bathed in pride as Estherly and her ballet classmates glided onto the stage. With each jeté, plié, pirouette, the Kaplan family nudged one another and clapped. When the ballet class danced offstage, my chorus line replaced them. Before leaving the wings, I rubbed the faux diamond Jewish star I was wearing around my neck. The charm was a birthday present I had requested after Ronnie's bar mitzvah, and one I turned to now for good luck. After my class danced together as a group, we were each awarded a solo.

When it was my turn in the spotlight, I sucked in my small tummy, then shuffled, hopped, stepped, flapped, and stepped—perfectly. Wearing the fixed smile our instructor insisted on, I focused on my family in the same row as Estherly's.

All eyes were upon me. Mother, Ronnie, and Dad,

whistling and clapping. As I hoofed, then bowed with a theatrical flourish, I decided this would be the end of my dance career. With such a limited time in the spotlight— after all those months of lessons and practice—and without my cousin as companion, it was time to toss the tap shoes and find a new project. What next? I thought to myself, still smiling optimistically at the audience, what next?

CHAPTER EIGHT

Mum's the Word

I was ten and a half in June of 1949 when Earl Lubin taught me how to sign. Earl, and his brother Rick, lived across the hall from us in our Division Street apartment building. Because they were best pals with my mother's four brothers—the Elkin boys—the Lubins seemed more like family than neighbors. At the time, all of our building's tenants called Earl "deaf and dumb," not aware this description was hurtful and untrue. But after Jane Wyman won an Academy Award for her performance as a deaf-mute in the film *Johnny Belinda,* we changed the "dumb" part, and Earl became "mute," too.

Earl was fitting his key into the front door of his flat, when I tapped him on the shoulder of his mustard-colored short-sleeved shirt to get his attention. "Please teach me sign language," I said—loud—after he turned at my touch. I tried acting out the words, looking to Earl, I suppose, like a character in a silent movie. He smiled at me from his pale, kind, broad face, and shrugged his shoulders to let me know my mimicking wasn't working. So I opened the door of our apartment, grabbed the number two pencil and

141

pad of paper we kept on the telephone table, and printed the question in block letters. Although I had beautiful cursive handwriting that won me an "E" in penmanship in Mrs. Lovejoy's fifth-grade class at Lafayette, I foolishly assumed Earl's speech and hearing problems demanded printing.

I wanted Earl to teach me sign language because I envied the graceful hand gestures he and his hearing brother Rick tossed at one another. Even when they argued, looking to me like jugglers with invisible props, I believed their darting fingers weren't as lethal as the shouting matches between my parents or the building's other warring couples.

While complaints, accusations, and Yiddish swear words barreled through many of our 12-flat's flimsy front doors, only silence and the occasional sounds of the radio flowed from the Lubins'. Sometimes, if I heard bickering coming from my apartment as I unlocked the door, I wished I could have reversed directions and entered the Lubins' sanctuary.

Another reason I wanted Earl to teach me sign language was that I was eager to see *Johnny Belinda,* and believed his lessons would help me better understand the film. The movie had premiered the year before at the Biltmore—a 1,750-seat Balaban & Katz theater five blocks away at Damen Avenue. Although my parents hadn't seen the film, I wasn't allowed to go when it first opened because Mother thought I was too young for serious drama and the movie house too expensive. Father concurred, saying

A poster for the movie Johnny Belinda *starring Jane Wyman and Lew Ayers. Wyman won an Academy Award for her role in the film that provided me with my first lesson in sex.*

the Biltmore was "too big and too far out of the neighbor-hood for my princess." Now, with me a whole year older, and the film due to open in two weeks at our 700-seat Vision Theater just a block away at Rockwell, my parents' objections were silenced. Since they still had no plans to see the film, I arranged to go with my friend Sandra Stein on the first Saturday it would be playing.

The day after I had asked Earl for lessons, he stopped in to see me in our store. I was in my sundries section, wear-ing my white apron and silently counting the coins in my cigar box register, when Earl handed me a sheet of paper. "Sign Language Alphabet and Common Phrases," it read. Before accepting his gift, I wiped my hands on the apron, careful that no *schmutz* should be transferred to his paper. I stared at the rows of fingers and thumbs that pointed up and down, curled, stood together, spread apart, and twisted into shapes. "Wow!" I said, excited to be offered such an intriguing new project—one that could possibly relieve the boredom of my grocery job.

I took the pencil I stowed behind my ear (just like Mother), and on the pad of paper I used to tally prices for occasional customers, printed: "THANKS. I'LL STUDY THIS AND PRACTICE. THEN WE CAN TALK TO EACH OTHER. O.K.?"

After one week of forming the alphabet and phrases in front of our bedroom mirror, I knocked on the Lubins' door—loud so Earl could feel the vibrations. When he an-

swered my drumming, I touched my lips with the fingertips
of my right hand, then moved it forward until the palm
faced up. "Thank you," I mouthed, repeating the phrase my
hand had just acted out. As he watched me move through
the entire sign language alphabet, Earl looked as pleased as
my teacher Mrs. Lovejoy had looked the day before, when I
recited *Hiawatha* by Henry Wadsworth Longfellow:

> *"On the shores of Gitche Gumme,*
> *Of the shining Big-Sea-Water,*
> *Stood Nokomis, the old woman, Pointing with*
> *   her finger westward,*
> *O'er the water pointing westward, To the purple*
> *   clouds of sunset."*

Dressed in a long-sleeved white blouse with a tight collar
and puffy sleeves, and a plaid skirt that had a shirred elastic
waist, I repeated the lines from memory while standing to
the right of my classroom desk. My place in Room 309 was
first row, first seat. I'm not certain I was there because I was
the shortest girl in the class, or because the teacher wanted
me near so she could hand me papers to pass out or notes
to deliver to the principal's office. At any rate, I appreciated
the position because it was easier for me to see the blackboard, which lately seemed blurrier and harder to read.

Although my eyesight often gave me trouble, I was
fortunate that my hearing "topped the charts," as the visiting school nurse had proclaimed during an annual exam.
Even when Mrs. Lovejoy turned her back to me, I had no
problem understanding what she was saying.

As I stood in my fifth-grade classroom reciting *Hiawatha*, Mrs. Lovejoy—tall and prim in a black suit covering a white blouse—beamed at me. I could hear whispers of "teacher's pet" behind my back, but pretended to be deaf and ignored my petty classmates. I was smug on that June day in 1949, and relished my place in Mrs. Lovejoy's heart. After all, she had chosen me, out of a class of 39 children, to accompany her the following Monday on a trip to a book warehouse to select new volumes for the school's library. Who cared about childish snickers if I could win that assignment?

Johnny Belinda had finally arrived at the Vision, and Sandra and I went to the show that Saturday. I thought Jane Wyman was terrific and sympathetic as Belinda, and that the gossiping Nova Scotia townspeople, who called her "the Dummy" behind her back, were cruel and ignorant. But the movie puzzled me: In one scary scene, when the music became spine-tingling, a character named Locky McCormick got drunk and tried to kiss Belinda when she was alone in her father's flour mill. Belinda looked terrified, the screen went black, and the next thing you knew, she was going to have a baby.

My smattering of sign language, and negligible knowledge of sex, didn't do a thing to help me figure out what had happened between Belinda and Locky in the fadeout, and how she had gotten pregnant (she named the baby boy "Johnny"). As we walked out of the movie, blinking in the bright sun, I was tempted to ask Sandra about it, but didn't want to sound dumb, so I decided to wait until I got home and ask my mother.

The minute I reached the store, I ran to the back where my mother was seated at the kitchen table, studying a stack of invoices. "How was the movie?" she asked without looking up.

"Good," I said. But before questioning her about Belinda, Locky, and the mysterious pregnancy, I gaped at the shelf to the left of the kitchen table. It was stacked with advertising flyers, unopened mail, old newspapers, paperback books with torn or missing covers, and other junk. "Where's my homework? Where's my permission slip for the book warehouse?" I cried. The day before, I had placed both important pieces of paper on the shelf to await a parent's review and signature. Now, they were drowning somewhere in the pile, surely soiled, possibly lost.

"They're in there somewhere," Mother answered, as she waved a hand in the direction of the shelf. "That's how your father puts things away. I try to keep things straight, but I give up with the shelf." My mother's usually pretty face now had a furrowed brow and down-turned mouth. Even her eyes—always a heart-stopping blue—took on an ordinary hue.

While I wanted my voice to be loud and forceful— to show the anger and hurt I was feeling—I curbed the volume because my mother looked as if she had enough *tsoris* without adding mine to the mix.

"Mommy, I need those papers. I'll get into trouble if I don't turn them in," I said flatly. "The book trip is Monday afternoon. If I don't bring the permission slip back the first thing in the morning, I won't be able to go."

"*Hak mir nisht in kop!* Your precious papers are in there somewhere. Keep looking. I asked you, how did you like the movie?"

My mother must have really been upset with the bills, I thought, if she turned to Yiddish to tell me to stop banging on her head. Although in America for 22 years, she—like my father and every other Jew on Division Street—used the old country's tongue to make a point. Early on, they spoke Yiddish if they wanted to keep their children in the dark. But soon enough, their swift *kinderlach* easily interpreted their meaning.

"The movie was fine," I said, as I picked through the debris. In my head, I berated my parents for their thoughtlessness. But in real life—in the store's kitchen—I kept still. Unlike my neighbor Earl, I had the power to speak and was hardly shy. In school, I was the first to volunteer to read aloud. But before my parents, when it came to expressing my feelings, my preference, I was mute. Why this childhood reticence? Did I sense my parents were overburdened—like the hopeless shelf—and want to spare them additional aggravation? Or perhaps, because I had witnessed so much bickering between the two of them and, imagining the pain their harsh words inflicted, wanted no part of conflict.

After sifting through the junky shelf and finally finding my homework and permission slip, I returned to the question I had planned to ask my mother earlier. "I don't understand something about the movie," I said.

"How did Belinda get pregnant and have a baby if she wasn't married?"

My mother turned her eyes from the bills and didn't say anything. She looked at me as if I were Sheldon Stern, the nebbish who sits in the last row, last seat, and always asks dumb questions, causing Mrs. Lovejoy to shake her head in exasperation.

"The things they show in the movies nowadays," Mother said, returning to the table and the red-inked bills. I considered staying put for an answer, but I was so glad to find my papers that I wanted to get them out of there and into my loose-leaf notebook before anything else bad could happen to them. I'll find someone else to explain it to me, I thought, and left the kitchen.

On the Monday afternoon that Mrs. Lovejoy and I entered the book warehouse on South Plymouth Court in Chicago's Loop, I felt as if I had landed in a fairy-tale kingdom. To me, this place was unbelievably beautiful, like Cinderella's ballroom, or Dorothy's Land of Oz. Boxes of books were stacked throughout the loft. All of the volumes were brand new, never-been-touched, covers clean, unsmudged. Sunlight that broke into the room through frosted windows sent beams of dusty light to the mountains of books, reminding me of illustrations of Moses and the Ten Commandments. This place is holy, I thought. I closed my eyes and inhaled the scent of paper stocks, inks, and paste bindings, which smelled as fragrant to me as the botanical garden in Humboldt Park.

As I walked through the aisles of books, I lifted out

Newbery and Caldecott award winners. I wiped my moist hands across my skirt before carefully turning their pages, then brought the books close to my face so it was easier to read the print. I used my fingertips to touch the golden seals that crowned each book: *McElligot's Pool, Stone Soup, Blueberries for Sal, Strawberry Girl, King of the Wind.* After making my suggestions to Mrs. Lovejoy, I continued to roam the aisles. I crossed my flat hands over my heart with the palms facing in. "I love you," I signed to the volumes spread before me—happy to have sign language to express my joy, for loud whoops would've been out of place in this temple.

When I returned home, after first stopping in our grocery store to let my parents know my whereabouts, I

My grade school portrait with my favorite teacher,
Mrs. Lovejoy. I'm seated in the first row, first seat on the right.

went upstairs to tell Earl about the book warehouse. Like Mrs. Lovejoy, Earl had become important to me that year. These two adults—who were not my parents—seemed to have more time for me than the two who were. My mother and father were so distracted by their struggling grocery business, Dad's overeating, and their contentious marriage, that they seemed to have little energy left for me. But I could always count on Earl to be happy to see me. This day, as I used sign language to describe my emotions at the book warehouse, Earl responded with gestures I could easily comprehend. Amazingly, we were conversing—sharing thoughts about the marvelous books I'd seen and his own collection.

Later that month, as my friend Sandra and I sat in the school's assembly hall waiting for the end-of-the-semester concert to begin, I brought up the subject of the mysterious pregnancy in *Johnny Belinda*. Although Sandra was a year older than I, and her class was seated a row ahead of mine, Mrs. Lovejoy gave me permission to take the empty seat next to my friend. "Because I don't have to keep my eye on you," she said.

The eighth-grade performance hadn't started yet, so I used the tumult caused by troops of children pounding down the aisles, rushing through the rows, and plopping into seats, to pursue the movie's mystery. "I can't believe you asked your mother," Sandra said, when I told her about my attempt. Then she patiently explained the blackout scene (that was the first time I had heard the word "rape") and also confirmed that you didn't have to be married to have a baby. "It's called 'out of wedlock,'" she said, with the wisdom of a sixth grader.

We stopped talking when the curtains parted and the eighth graders took their places on stage. I could make out their forms but from this distance wasn't able to discern faces or expressions. "Let me see your glasses," I said to Sandra. My girlfriend had curly blonde hair and a cute smile, and with her spectacles on, looked serious and smart. She removed them from her face and handed them to me. "Wow!" I said. "You can see everything with these." I was jealous. If my sight could be as sharp as my hearing, imagine what a super brain I could be. Instead of just reading books like those I stroked in the warehouse, maybe I could grow up to be an author with my own name imprinted on a book cover.

As the students sang and danced on stage, I continued to turn to Sandra and tap her on the shoulder of her starched white blouse with, "Please, your glasses." With her lenses, a bright new world opened: Each child on stage was separate from the next, blouses bore patterns, ribbons and barrettes enlivened hairstyles, the boys' ties were thin or wide, shoes had laces or buckles. As I marveled at this improvement in my vision, Mrs. Lovejoy came to our aisle. "Elaine Shapiro," she said to me, hands on hips, eyes narrowed, mouth a straight line. "I'm surprised at you. Talking in assembly. Stop it right now."

"Mrs. Lovejoy," I started to say, wanting to explain the once-blurry stage and the now-sharp details. But she stopped me with a finger to her lips, a sign I immediately understood. I sank low in my seat and heard giggles from my classmates in the rows behind. I was devastated. I had never been scolded by a teacher before, and especially not by Mrs. Lovejoy. Although school was due to end for the semester, I was going to be in her class again in September for 6B. What if she remembered the assembly scene and forgot all of my excellent 5A schoolwork and deeds?

When the assembly ended, I joined my classmates and kept my head down, my thoughts ricocheting between Mrs. Lovejoy's reprimand and the forbidden words Sandra had taught me earlier.

"Let's go, children," Mrs. Lovejoy said, guiding us out the double doors. As I passed her by, she put a hand on my drooping shoulder and said, "Have a good summer, dear." I lifted my head, my eyes still shining from earlier tears. But instead of talking and risking another warning, I touched my lips with the fingertips of my flat right hand, then moved it forward until the palm faced up. Next, I crossed my hands over my heart with the palms facing in. "Thank you" and "I love you," I mouthed as my fingers spelled out my gratitude.

My stupidity about *Johnny Belinda* didn't stop me, the summer of that year, from having my first crush—it was on Ben Levinson, the oldest son of my mother's friend, Rose. That's why, when Mrs. Levinson invited me to join her on a trip to North Avenue Beach with her three sons, I thought I was the luckiest girl on Division Street.

"I don't know, Rose," my mother said, after Mrs. Levinson issued her invitation. I was helping out in our store bagging groceries, substituting for my 14-year-old brother Ronnie who was away that summer at Camp Henry Horner. Mother hesitated about the beach because a month earlier, she had read in the *Chicago Sun-Times* that "seven new polio victims were added to hospital rolls making the total of 180 the worst Infantile Paralysis epidemic in the area this year."

"Don't be such a worrier, Min," Mrs. Levinson said as she stood in the doorway of our store. "That was in Texas. Nothing's going to happen to your baby."

Looking like a glamourpuss with one hand on the doorframe and the other at her waist, Mrs. Levinson was wearing a head scarf over her blonde curls, and sunglasses, and the straps of her bathing suit peeked from her sleeveless blouse. "If it was bad in Chicago, they'd close the pools and beaches," she said.

I kept my mouth shut, but to tell the truth, I was worried about infantile paralysis, too. When newsreels at the Vision Theater issued warnings about the plague, I imagined my own childish legs or arms stiff and cold like the meat in Dad's walk-in freezer. I conjured pitiful scenes with me hobbling in September to sixth grade, bound by leg braces, or being pushed in a wheelchair by my solemn-faced older brother. Or worse yet, I saw myself motionless in an iron lung, deaf and mute like Sleeping Beauty— except my villain would have been a fast-spreading virus, not an evil fairy's curse.

But I was willing to risk the disease if it meant an afternoon spent with Ben. Fourteen to my almost 11, Ben had eyes the color of the lake we'd soon be visiting. And now in the summer, the sun he adored had bleached his curly brown hair golden and tinted his skin silky beige. But besides his good looks—and wrestler-like build that reminded me of my father—there was something else that drew me to him. Ben was different from the other neighborhood boys. He was more intense, mysterious, impenetrable.

I told no one of my crush on Ben, but would write in my diary, "I saw Ben in Humboldt Park today. I think he smiled at me, but I'm not sure." Lying on my bed, I'd draw our names encased in a heart, or write "Mrs. Ben Levinson" over and over on a blank page.

When Mom finally gave me permission to go to the beach, I raced upstairs to grab my bathing suit. Earl was exiting and locking the door of his apartment, and when he saw me panting, signed, "Where are you rushing to?"

"To the beach," I answered, grateful to use my hands as I was out of breath from my sprint. Then I watched as he signed an unfamiliar phrase: First, he formed both hands into the symbol for "K." Keeping his hands together, he moved them forward, down, back, and up in a circular movement. His facial expression was the clue that he had just warned me, "Be careful."

After retrieving my suit from the dresser drawer and putting it on under my clothing, I debated about taking my eyeglasses. I had told my mother about the school assembly and clearer stage with Sandra's spectacles (I omitted the part about Mrs. Lovejoy's reproof), so she took me to Busch's Opticians for an exam. For $7—50 cents down and 50 cents weekly—I got a diagnosis of nearsightedness, plus a pair of shell rim glasses. The thick lenses cleared up my vision problems, but I balked at wearing them because they hid my pretty green eyes. Although I didn't want Ben to see me in the glasses, I took the pair with me because I wanted to read the *True Romance* magazines I was taking to the beach. I'll put them on when he's in the water, I told myself.

With one hand on the banister and the other carrying the straw bag that held my magazines and eyeglasses, and with my feet in barely buckled sandals, I raced two at a time down the stairs and out the door to meet Mrs. Levinson. She was clutching a brown paper shopping bag filled with supplies for our outing: suntan lotion, peanut butter and jelly sandwiches, apples, and comic books. Ben was carrying several scratchy, mustard-colored woolen blankets from the Army-Navy surplus store. Sam, the middle Levinson son, held two thermos jugs of purple Kool-Aid. Allan, the youngest, swung plastic pails and shovels.

The two younger boys wore T-shirts with "Bucking Bronco" printed on their fronts—Ben's was plain white— and all wore cotton shorts in various summer shades.

When the streetcar pulled up at our corner, the three Levinson boys leapt onto the tread, passed the conductor with a wave over their shoulders, and yelled, "Ma's got the money." Then, they rushed to the rear of the car, flipped the backrests of two cane seats over so they'd face east, and tussled over who'd get the windows.

"Knock it off, boys," Mrs. Levinson said, as she handed the conductor carfare for the five of us. She and I sat together, I at the window, she on the aisle, both of us placid in our mother-daughter pretense. As the streetcar moved along the tracks, I stared out the window. When I spotted a young couple pointing to an item in a jewelry store window, I imagined they were Ben and I selecting a diamond for our future engagement. Although my sweetheart was sitting several rows ahead in the trolley, I could almost feel his bare arm next to mine, and blushed at the stirrings the fancied touch had fueled.

As the streetcar reached the end of the line, about three miles from home, we still had a six-block steamy trudge to the lakefront. I almost regretted arriving at our destination because it meant the finale of my daydreams. But as soon as I saw the pretend smokestacks of North Avenue Beach's boathouse, I was eager for the *mecheich*

The North Avenue Beach boathouse as it appears today.
The Art Moderne structure was designed by Chicago Park
District architect Emanuel V. Buchsbaum as part of President
Roosevelt's federal job program. Renee S. Elkin Photography.

(pleasure) the cool lake would offer. The sleek boathouse had been built 10 years earlier as part of President Roosevelt's federal job program. A Park District architect of the time, Emanuel V. Buchsbaum, designed the Art Moderne boathouse to look like a graceful ocean liner. It was painted blue and white, and along with the smokestacks, the boathouse had a flat roof, porthole windows, and an open walkway that ringed the ship.

At the gangplank, we all removed our shoes, then skipped barefooted across frying sand until we found spots for our blankets. After unloading her shopping bag, Mrs. Levinson settled on one blanket, Allan claimed a place in the sand for digging, and Sam and Ben raced into the lake, shouting as the chilly water knifed their bare skin.

After shedding my playclothes and before tiptoeing in, I put my eyeglasses on to see where the lifeguard was stationed. A suntanned adolescent in red Park District bathing trunks ("visible for miles" according to a story in the newspaper announcing the start of beach season) stood at the foot of his wooden perch. He was chatting with a teenage girl in a two-piece bathing suit, but kept one hand on the whistle around his neck. Although the lifeguard was at his post, I was troubled he wasn't scanning the lake. I didn't know how to swim and was afraid of deep water, but I quashed my anxiety, placed my glasses inside my bag, and tiptoed over sand, stones, shells, and dead fish. "On the shores of Gitche Gumme, On the shining Big-Sea-Water," I recited, believing the Longfellow poetry would ease my mind. I halted when the water level reached my waist and was splashing happily in my comfort zone when Ben crept up behind me. Without a word, he put his wide hand atop my skull and pressed my head deep under the water. I struggled to pop up and managed to catch my breath. But instead of stopping at what I thought was horseplay, he pressed down again, pushing me under, below the water's surface. Like a scene straight out of the movies, I came up for air, choking and coughing water from my nose and windpipe. My heart was pounding in my ears, as Ben—who was likely double my weight—again and again pressed my head under the water. And again and again, I struggled to come up. I tried to say "Stop!" but unable to speak with a mouth full of lake water, I brought the little finger of my right hand down at right angles on my left palm, hoping Ben understood sign language. But he ignored this, just as he had my voiced pleas.

With his face close to mine, Ben reminded me of Locky McCormick, and at once I understood the panic Belinda must have felt when the movie screen went black. This was not rape—this much I knew—but I still feared for my life.

So this is what drowning is like, I thought, as I slipped under the water. Believing my fate was out of my hands, I ceased to struggle. It was quiet below the surface, like the silence in Earl's apartment. I closed my eyes and mental images floated past me like sea creatures: This is worse than polio. My mother will never forgive Rose. I'll never get to see Mrs. Lovejoy in sixth grade. I'll wind up stiff and mute in a coffin at Weinstein Brothers' Funeral Home.

At last, Mrs. Levinson spotted us from her blanket. "Ben, cut it out!" she yelled, racing into the water, the splashes bouncing against her trim thighs. As her eldest son removed his beefy hand from the top of my head, he said to his mother, "I was only playing." Lifting me up out of the water with one hand tight around my upper arm, Ben leaned close to me. His wet cheek touched mine—a move I had daydreamed about—as he said, "You're such a crybaby." He released my sore arm, pushed me towards the shore, then leapt into the surf to join his younger brother. Mrs. Levinson placed a sunburned arm around my waist, and held me close to her as I continued to cough out water. When we reached our blankets, I retrieved my glasses and put them on, not caring what I looked like, just happy to be alive. Now, I could see the lifeguard, who was still gabbing with the girl, and I could even make out Ben. This boy I once loved, and now hated, looked to me like a *bulvan* as he bellowed and stampeded through the waves.

Seated together on her blanket, Mrs. Levinson wrapped a beach towel around my quivering shoulders and gathered me to her.

While I welcomed her comfort, I didn't have the nerve to tell this woman I adored that I was afraid of her oldest son and wouldn't be joining her at the beach anymore. But I was certain my mother's best friend—like my neighbor Earl who caught my voiceless words—understood exactly what was in my heart.

NINE

——◦৲৹◦——

Are You Now,
or Have You Ever Been . . .

His name was Tony and he sat in the last row, last seat of my sixth-grade classroom at Lafayette Grammar School. He wasn't the brightest nor the dumbest boy in our grade, but as soon as I learned his name was Tony—so much more lyrical and exotic than the more familiar Sheldons, Marshalls, or Melvins—I was intrigued.

Tony's last name escapes me now, but I know it ended in an "A," just like Sinatra, who was my favorite crooner in 1950, the year I turned 12. It could have been my crush on Frank Sinatra that spilled on to Tony, for I had mooned over the singer ever since I first heard him on the radio. And when I saw Sinatra's skinny, vulnerable self on Bob Hope's television special, *The Star Spangled Revue,* I was hooked.

On the May 31st evening of Sinatra's appearance, my family was seated in our living room focusing on our new RCA Victor table model TV. My dad had gone to Goldblatt's on Chicago and Ashland to purchase the $375 set—for $43 down—after my 15-year-old brother and I had wheedled him and my mom with, "Everybody in the building has one." This was false; only one out of every 10 Americans had TV sets at the time, and I doubt all of the tenants of our aging building could afford this new medium. Our parents succumbed because they wanted to watch *The Texaco Star Theatre* with Milton Berle, *Your Show of Shows* with Sid Caesar, and *The Goldbergs*—three programs made more entertaining because their stars were Jewish.

I think my mother had a special bond with *The Goldbergs* ever since my *bubbie,* Sophie Elkin, had died the year before. I imagine Gertrude Berg's character reminded my mother of her own beloved *Yiddishe momme.*

On the night my family watched Sinatra's first television appearance, my parents sank into the sagging cushions of our upholstered couch, while Ronnie and I sat cross-legged on the carpet—the recommended six feet from the television screen. As Sinatra sang, *"I'm gonna love you, like nobody's loved you, Come rain or come shine,"* I ignored eye doctors' warnings and scooted closer to the set, certain the young man from Hoboken—with the name that wasn't Jewish—was sending the song directly to my preteen heart.

It wasn't that I didn't like being Jewish. After all, I admired our tribe's celebrities, scientists, and authors; and I couldn't get enough of my mother's schmaltz-heavy cooking. And there was a certain comfort in being surrounded by others like myself. But at times, I felt constrained in the close-knit Jewish neighborhood we lived in, and longed to know what was on the other side.

Tony showed interest in me earlier that week. I was in the schoolyard at the time, waiting for the bell to ring and humming a Sinatra song, when Tony came up and playfully cuffed my arm. "How did you get to be such a brain?" was his opening remark. I was surprised by his attention, because with his black hair brushed back into a ducktail, blue eyes circled by long lashes, olive skin, and pretty smile, he was a dreamboat. And to be honest, there was nothing special about me. I wasn't the prettiest or the ugliest girl in class, but I was the shortest. My black hair had body, and when I wasn't wearing my thick glasses, you could say I had nice green eyes.

I did have an outgoing personality, but I wasn't "fast" like a few of the girls who applied Hazel Bishop Tangee lipstick in the girls' bathroom. And my chest was flat—no buds had sprouted yet to warrant a visit to the lingerie department of Marshall Field's for a first bra fitting.

Maybe Tony was curious about this good little Jewish girl simply because I was different from him, or perhaps he was buttering me up to borrow my homework. Whatever the reason, Tony waited after class each day and walked me part of the way home until our paths diverged. On these strolls, we talked about our favorite movies and television shows—he liked gangsters and war stories, and I preferred comedy and romance—but we never discussed books because reading wasn't one of Tony's favorite subjects.

At night in our apartment, as my family watched their favorite television programs, I'd stretch my arms and yawn,

feigning sleepiness so that I could turn in early and fanta-
size about my crush. I remember vowing in those noctur-
nal moments: "This is not puppy love. This is real love."

A few days after Sinatra's first television appearance, Tony
and I were dawdling in the school's third-floor hallway,
when he made a bold overture. "How about going to Riverview with me next Tuesday?" he asked. "It's a school holiday and Two Cents Day."

I was leaning against a bulletin board and thumb-
tacks were denting the back of my blouse, causing some
pain but not enough to move me away. As I considered
Tony's offer, I took in the portrait I had been sketching in
my head each night: his rakish hairstyle, adorable grin,
and lips that could have been Sinatra's. I could also smell
garlic, a mouthwatering scent that in my family's store was
married to kosher deli, but at Lafayette signaled Tony.

I hesitated a response—not because I wasn't ecstatic
to be asked to go to Chicago's popular amusement park
with this lovely Italian boy, but because I was trying to figure out how I'd ever get my parents' permission. Besides
me being not quite 12, which my mother and father believed too young to think about boys, Tony was a *shaygitz,*
not one of our own kind. And although I had never heard
either of my parents bad-mouth our Italian customers, I
understood that if and when I would be allowed to date, it
would be with "a nice Jewish boy."

"Go to Riverview with you?" I repeated, stalling for
time. When Tony nodded "yes," I replied, "I'd love to." To
myself I thought, how am I going to pull this off?

*Chicago's Riverview Amusement Park was one of the most
popular and famous parks in the world. After 64 seasons,
it closed its doors in 1967. Photo courtesy of
Sharpshooters Productions, Inc.*

I couldn't concentrate on schoolwork the rest of the
afternoon, as my mind bounced from my acceptance of
Tony's proposal to the upcoming third degree before my
parents. As I stood in line for the girls' bathroom, a familiar voice pulled me back to earth.

"What's the matter with you? I've been calling your
name and you didn't turn around." It was my new best
friend, Ruth Rosenfeld Ross, who had slipped in line behind me.

When I did twist to see her, I had to look a good
10 inches above my head, for Ruth was one of the tallest
girls in our class. She and her mother, Selma, had recently
arrived in Chicago from New Jersey after first escaping
Nazi-occupied Poland. When our teacher introduced this

long-legged, dark-haired refugee to our class, I was awed by her height—a giant compared to my own short stature—and also by her intelligence. Schooled in stricter European classrooms, this new girl with a foreign accent was far brighter than the average Chicago public school student.

Ruth was intrigued by my size, too, and years later she told me, "You were like a doll I could put on my lap." Along with our love for reading—especially books that featured handsome hoodlums like Frank Abbott in *The Amboy Dukes* and Nick Romano in *Knock on Any Door*—we quickly became best buddies.

Little by little, on our visits to each other's homes, or on our placid walks to the Humboldt Park Library on California Avenue, I learned about the dangerous journey that had brought her and her mother to America in November of 1949. "We posed as Gentiles," Ruth had told me on one of our outings, "and it was my mother's quick thinking that saved us from capture. In all those terrible years, we believed that once the war was over and the Nazis were defeated, Europe's remaining Jews would be hailed as heroes."

She had been telling me this as we stood in the library's checkout line. We had watched the bored clerk press the date stamp into an inkpad, her ashen hair and pale complexion making her look as if she rarely left the stacks. The clerk then removed date cards from the inside flap of our hardcover books, stamped the cards, and slipped them back into the safety of their paper pockets. With the soft snap of covers being closed, Ruth continued, "I pictured us Jewish survivors being carried on people's shoulders, like we were celebrities. I was sure we would be honored for what we had endured, for our bravery. But it never happened." Shaking her head in disgust, she said, "We were DPs to you Americans—displaced persons— there never was any cheering."

I felt guilty when my best friend had told me this, for the only sacrifice I could remember during the war was that I couldn't get bubble gum. Ruth's life-threatening experiences and youthful courage, contrasted with my snug life on Division Street, often made me feel tinier than I really was.

"Elaine, why are you ignoring me?" Ruth now asked as we stood in line to the girls' bathroom.

"I'm sorry, I didn't hear you," I said, inching up forward to the stalls. "I'm trying to figure something out." Up till now, I had hidden my romance from my best friend. Because she took a different route home, Ruth hadn't witnessed Tony and me on our after-school ambles. I felt guilty for deceiving her, but I had the feeling Ruth would have the same objections to Tony as my parents. But now, with his invitation in the air, I couldn't keep quiet any longer.

"You know Tony," I asked, "that cute guy who sits in the last row, last seat? He invited me to go to Riverview with him next week."

"The *shaygitz*?" Ruth said.

"He's Italian."

"So, what's wrong with Jewish?"

"Nothing's wrong with Jewish. It's just that Tony asked me."

"And you're thinking of going? Are you *meshugga*? Your parents will kill you."

Ruth's reaction confirmed my fears. If I wanted to blissfully stroll the Riverview midway with Tony, crush myself next to his slim Italian body in a roller coaster, watch him toss at a target to win me a panda bear, and taste sticky sweet cotton candy as it dissolved on my tongue, I'd have to lie. This would be difficult, I knew, for except for some harmless fibs—"It wasn't me who ate the last piece of strudel," or "Yes, Ma, the corduroy skirt is pretty"—I never lied to my parents, or rebelled in any way. Now, I could barely recognize this new me, this brazen girl coolly contemplating a deception that could break my parents' hearts, but also make mine sing.

After school that day, when I entered our store, my mother was dusting some canned goods that were lined up on a shelf. Except for a radio news program announcing the number of U.S. military lost in the Korean War, there was no other sound in the place.

"Hi, honey," Mom said, turning her rouged cheek to catch my kiss. I stared at the cans of Libby's, Savoy's, and Campbell's. In playful moods, I imagined them to be soldiers standing at attention, waiting for General MacArthur's review. I saw their brightly colored labels as war medals. But unlike men engaged in combat, our store's tin soldiers hardly moved, rarely left their posts on the shelf, never were set "at ease." Month after month they stood, their expiration dates coming dangerously close. Poor peas, peaches, and pineapple chunks in heavy syrup, I would think, forsaken by customers who are now pushing carts along supermarket aisles, or shopping in new neighborhoods far from Division Street.

"Ma," I said, turning from my illusion and placing my schoolbooks on her counter, "a bunch of kids from my class are going to Riverview on Tuesday. It's a 'teachers' something or other day,' so we're off and we can get into the park for two cents." As I chatted, trying to appear nonchalant, I lifted another cloth from the rag pile and joined my mother in the dusting. Helpful and considerate, the better to relax her guard, I thought.

"Who's going?"

I was prepared for this line of questioning, and offered up six names of Jewish classmates. For good measure, I tossed in more girls than boys, lest my mother worry there would be any pairing. She stopped her chore, turned sideways, and studied my face. As her blue eyes scanned my green ones, I could feel her weighing, "Can I trust her?"

I could also feel my guilt multiplying. How can I deceive this woman that I love—this motherless daughter, who likely never betrayed my grandmother? Doesn't my mother have enough sadness without my lies? But one thought of my Italian Tony and his Sinatra-like *punim,* and the possibility of holding his hot hand as we sidestepped Riverview's crowds, sealed my lips as tightly as those whom I had seen testify before Senator Joseph McCarthy earlier that year.

I remember cringing as my family watched the House Un-American Activities Committee hearings that were being televised. As the senator's, "Are you now, or have you ever been . . ." questioning reverberated in our living room, I feared for the Hollywood 10—screenwriters and directors, many of whom were Jewish—as they faced the diabolical McCarthy. Although a young girl at the time, I understood how McCarthy's Communist witch hunt was destroying careers. Such courage, I would think as I watched those who refused "to name names." Could I ever be as brave as my clansmen who stood up to injustice?

The afternoon I betrayed my mother, she listened as I provided the false list of Jewish friends bound for River-view. Satisfied I would be in safe, good company, she gave her okay. When the Tuesday of my date with Tony rolled around, I was allowed to travel on my own to the park where I supposedly was going to meet up with my school friends. A one-block walk to Western Avenue, then a three-mile streetcar ride to Belmont would be manageable for this responsible, trustworthy girl, my parents reasoned.

When I arrived at the gate, Tony was waiting at the gaudy entrance. Dwarfed by the giant archway with mina-rets at each side, my swain looked like the kewpie doll I hoped he'd win for me. The calliope sounds of the carou-sel, shouts of "Wait up!" and the clanking gears of carni-val rides met me, too. "Hi," Tony said, taking my hand in his. "You look pretty."

It was a hot day, so I had convinced my mother that my white batiste cotton midriff blouse with an eyelet ruf-fle would be appropriate clothing. When I had exited our grocery store, the elastic top of the blouse sat demurely on my shoulders, but by the time Tony laid eyes on me, I had pushed the ruffle down two inches.

"Thanks," I said. "You look nice, too." Tony was wearing a short-sleeved, button-down shirt and I could see a gold cross dangling from his neck. Why hadn't I noticed the religious symbol before, I asked myself. Was the cross hidden beneath polo shirts, or was I so blinded by adoration that I missed it? Now, with my guilt clinging to me like my damp cotton blouse, I stared at the jewelry and pictured my parents wailing into their stained aprons—"*oy gevalts*" punctuating their tears. But once again, Tony's sweet smile, warm hand, and mellow voice pushed my parents' heart-wrenching images back behind the counters of our store.

As Tony and I strolled among the crowd of mostly white adults and school kids, my mouth watered with the smell of cotton candy, ice cream cones, and hotdogs that passersby were munching as they lined up for rides. I noticed there were a few more black youngsters at Riverview than I had seen on previous visits. Although none of the students at my grammar school were black, I had overheard some concern about the topic the week before in our grocery store:

"You know the *schvartzees* that got the *gelt* are moving out of the slums," Mrs. Bronstein had said. This customer was around my mother's age, but unlike my slim, stylish mother, Mrs. Bronstein was fat, with messy salt-and-pepper colored hair. Although she had been in America as long as my parents, Mrs. Bronstein looked as if she had just gotten off the boat from Russia. Sweat had stained her blouse, and a washed-out slip showed past her wrinkled skirt. Her son Melvin was in my class at Lafayette. And like both his parents, Melvin was *schlubby*. His fleshy body, small eyes, and squeaky voice often reminded me of a cartoon pig.

"Who can blame the colored?" my father had said, taking a drag from his cigarette. He leaned his head back, blew out a puff of smoke, coughed, and continued: "Jammed into those firetrap kitchenette apartments, rats crawling on their kids. I'd want to get the hell out of there, too." My father, like the Bronsteins, was overweight, but the clothing he wore under his bloodstained apron was clean and pressed.

I heard my mother say softly, "Some of our own people are slumlords. It's a *shonda* [shame] on all of our heads."

I'm not sure if Mr. Bronstein, who had accompanied his spouse, caught my mother's comment, but he interjected, "Before you know it, the *schvartzees* will be on Division Street." In his rumpled shirt that flopped outside his pants, the husband looked a match to his wife.

"Somebody's got to rent the vacant apartments," my mother said, forcefully now, as she wrote the Bronsteins' total in her ledger book. "Look around. As soon as people can afford it, they're out of here. To Albany Park, like my sister Mollie, or to the suburbs like my cousin Lil."

"Such a big talker," Mrs. Bronstein sniffed. "I don't see your precious son going to Tuley High School. Too many Spanish, too many *schvartzees* for him?"

"He just wanted to be with his friends," my mother had said, slapping the ledger book shut. "They're all in Albany Park now, so he used Mollie's address to get into Roosevelt. Big deal."

I didn't enter the conversation, but I was familiar

with the topic because we had discussed it recently in my social studies class. Our teacher, Miss Thompson, had explained about Chicago's Black Belt between 12th and 79th Street and Wentworth and Cottage Grove Avenue. Looking serious in a two-piece gray suit and sensible shoes, she told us about the second great migration of blacks from the South after World War II. "Machines began to take the place of laborers in the cotton and tobacco fields, and Chicago's stockyards and steel industry provided an opportunity for them," she had said, as she pointed to a map she had rolled down like a window shade.

One of the boys in class, Ralph was his name, raised his hand and asked, "How come the colored got so many kids and run down the neighborhoods?"

I had gasped, along with some of the others who were taught to keep the lid on prejudice. "You shouldn't talk like that, Ralph," Miss Thompson had said and released the map so it snapped shut like a shotgun blast. "Most of your own parents are from the old country, from big families. The Negroes who are moving to Chicago are just like your parents, they want a better life for their children. When your relatives came to this country they had the benefit of relief organizations that helped them get on their feet. But Negroes from the South don't have the same support system."

"Whatever," Ralph had said of her lecture. Then, under his breath so that only the kids closest to him could hear, "They had just better stay out of my neighborhood."

"So where to? Aladdin's Castle, the Tilt-a-Whirl, Shoot-the-Chutes, the Bobs?" It was Tony's voice waking me from my somber reverie, and I was back on the light-hearted midway of Riverview Amusement Park. I was relieved he had omitted the Old Mill Tunnel-of-Love, because the thought of the darkened cave, and the moans of tangled couples in slow-moving boats surrounding us with their smooching, was scary. I may have been bold enough to deceive my mother, but this passageway called for skills and courage I hadn't yet mastered.

"Not Aladdin's Castle," I said, as we stood before the huge wooden portrait of a turbaned man that served as the castle's entrance. With his wide scary eyes and fiendish glare, Aladdin reminded me of Senator McCarthy. Besides that, I didn't want Tony to view me in the funhouse mirrors that made me look squat and fat—like someone I hoped I'd never be.

"The Bobs," I said. "Let's go on the Bobs."

"You're not scared of roller coasters?" he asked, a look of respect lighting up his olive-colored face.

"No, I like them," I said. I wasn't insulted Tony had thought me too timid for the wild ride—I was surprised at myself as well. For a girl who had been afraid to sleep next to the bedroom window just a few years earlier, I had blossomed into someone who loved roller coasters. Their sharp curves, shortened dips, and perpendicular climbs and drops thrilled me. I liked the Comet and the Blue Streak, too, but the Bobs was my favorite, and I would happily scream with the rest of the jostled riders as we'd screech recklessly along the roller coaster's tracks.

On the way to the Bobs, we paused at an attraction that had always made me feel queasy. Its posted sign read,

"Dunk Bozo the Clown." In this game of chance, contestants paid to throw balls at a target that, when hit, would release a man into a tank of water. The men who took turns sitting on swings suspended above the tank were black, and they would drop into the water below if the pitcher hit his mark. This game typically drew crowds of young, white toughs eager to purchase balls. Although the light- and dark-haired boys seemed to be of different ethnic backgrounds, at this game, with ammunition in their tight fists, they bonded as "white people."

"Let's go," I said to Tony, pulling his hand away to move us from the mob. "I can't watch." Ever since I read about the rioting that erupted in Chicago the year before when blacks tried to move into the white neighborhoods of Park Manor and Englewood, I was more sympathetic to the race. Also, I put myself in their place because my people faced restrictive covenants, too. It was hard to swallow, but Jews were unwanted in certain parts of the city.

"Just a minute," Tony said, standing firm. "Let me see one toss."

I was frightened of this bunch, whom I knew called the game "Dunk the Nigger." But the black men on Riverview's swings weren't intimidated by the pitchers' slurs, and taunted the white boys to encourage more rounds. Egged on by their racist buddies, more than a few pitchers deliberately missed the target and threw the ball directly at the black men.

I watched Tony's face as his eyes flashed from the white thrower to the black man on the swing. Please don't ask to play, I said to myself, for I couldn't bear the sight of my barely won boyfriend turning into a bigot. As a tat-tooed pitcher wound up, Tony kept silent and squeezed my hand in his, looking as serious as Richard Widmark in the movie *Kiss of Death*.

The ride on the Bobs was just as I had pictured. At the start, Tony and I sat rigid, our hands on the bar in front of us, our eyes fastened on the upcoming hill. But after the first deep drop, we scrunched up against one another. Tony left one hand on the bar and wrapped the other around my bare shoulder. After several trips ("Only 5 Cents To Ride Again!"), we stumbled off the roller coaster. As we walked hand in hand to the Pair-A-Chutes, I heard a familiar screechy voice behind us. "Well, hel-lo, Elaine. And hel-lo, Tony." It was our classmate Melvin Bronstein.

His small eyes darted from my face, to my off-the-shoulder blouse, to Tony's Italian face, and to our entwined hands. I quickly untangled my fingers and said, "Hi." Tony narrowed his eyes, but didn't say a word.

"Have fun," Melvin said, in a voice more like a threat than a blessing. "See ya back home." Then he turned and ran towards the exit. Was he racing to tell my parents about my *shaygitz* boyfriend? I better get home and con-fess before the pig has a chance to blab, I thought. Maybe honesty will bring a lighter sentence.

"This has to be the last ride," I said to Tony.

"No problem."

I grasped the ropes attached to the parachute seat while the ride lifted me 212 feet up to a tower. I freed one hand to touch the Jewish star I wore around my neck.

Closing my eyes, I prayed, "Keep me safe," more for my homecoming than the drop to come. The seat swayed as it poised at the top of the tower and in the thinner air of the carnival ride I felt lightheaded. I glanced at Tony, separate and fearless in the seat next to me. Unlike my worried face, Tony's was alive with excitement. Instead of grabbing the ropes for dear life as I was doing, Tony's arms were spread wide and he rocked his seat to make his position even more dangerous.

The parachute suddenly dropped and my stomach flipped over and over until the ride slowed in its last feet of descent. Tony and I unbuckled ourselves from the protective harnesses and walked silently to the park's exit. At the streetcar stop, Tony bent down and kissed me on the cheek. "I had fun," he said.

I touched the spot his Sinatra lips had marked. "Me too," I said, as the Western Avenue streetcar pulled up. "See you in school." Sweating in the trolley, with my forehead pressed against the window, I thought about Tony and composed a speech I would offer my parents. "There's this boy in school, he's very nice," and continue listing invented virtues. And when they would ask the inevitable, "Is he Jewish?" I would bravely tell the truth.

After arriving home, with the elastic of my blouse now up over my shoulders, I walked into our store, head as high as the Hollywood 10, brave as my tall friend Ruth, ready to face my inquisitors. But the sight of my two parents standing with their arms crossed in front of them—in an unusual pose of togetherness—warned me that Melvin had beaten me to it. Before I had a chance to utter one syllable of my rehearsed speech, my parents said in unison, "You're not seeing the Italian again."

As much as I adored Tony, I loved my parents more, and knew I could never defy or hurt them. With our grocery store's dim prospects, my mother's loss of her *Yiddishe momme,* my dad's chancy health, and their quarrelsome marriage, they had *genug tsoris* (enough worries) without adding a rebellious daughter to the mix.

"Okay," I said, all bravery evaporating into the store's stifling air.

The next day in school, I was prepared to tell Tony good-bye, but he was absent. Days went by without his appearance. Then Ruth reported what was on the grapevine: Tony had been joyriding in a stolen car, got kicked out of Lafayette, and was shipped to Montefiore—the public school for troubled youth. When I heard this, I felt a mixture of sadness and relief. Sad because this small, brainy Jewish girl was not thrilling enough to lure Tony from petty crime.

And relief, for without Tony's swaggering presence, my remaining journey at Lafayette—though ordinary and predictable—would be easier to navigate for a girl ill-suited to danger.

For the time being, I'd have to confine my crush to Sinatra, and any desired thrills to the roller coaster rides of Riverview.

Old Soldiers Never Die

The first time I learned our grocery store had lost its battle, was on Thursday, April 19, 1951, one day before the Jewish holiday of Passover. It was late in the afternoon, and I was in my sundries section of the store staring out the plate glass window. A Green Hornet streetcar was paused

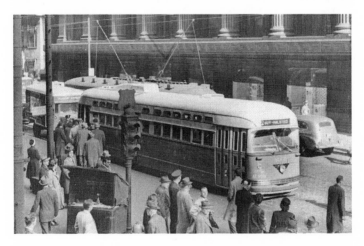

This is the type of Green Hornet streetcar, sleek and modern at the time, that replaced aging red Pullmans on Division Street. Courtesy of the Chicago Transit Authority.

on the corner, and the trolley made me realize how much my Division Street landscape had changed over the years. With its lime-and-white glaze, the Green Hornet looked fresh and sleek, unlike the red Pullmans it had replaced— the ones now fading in car barns. I noticed, too, that several more of the ground floor shops across the street were either vacant or operated by strangers.

Although there were no customers to wait on, my parents were still wearing their store aprons—once bright white—now stained and shadowy from daily hand swipes and laundering. Mom was behind her counter, studying the open pages of her ledger book. Dad was on the other side. He rested his elbows on the marble surface and his right foot atop a wooden crate of seltzer bottles—careful to avoid the untouched stacks of Silvercup white bread and Rosen's rye the bakery man brought in that morning.

"Old soldiers never die, they just fade away," Dad said.

"What are you talking about?" Mom asked, looking up from her columns.

"MacArthur. His speech. Didn't you hear it? They're discussing it again on the news."

Intrigued, I left my shelves of toothpaste, aspirin, and chewing gum to join my parents at the radio. When Dad turned up the volume, we could heard the announcer describe General Douglas MacArthur's farewell speech to Congress.

Eight days earlier, on April 11th, President Harry Truman had replaced MacArthur in Korea because the general went over the president's head and wrote letters to the

Veterans of Foreign Wars and the Speaker of the House about launching an aggressive campaign against China.

My parents and I were silent as the announcer read MacArthur's words: "I am closing my fifty-two years of military service. When I joined the Army even before the turn of the century, it was the fulfillment of all my boyish hopes and dreams." And then the announcer repeated the line that Dad had just said, "Old soldiers never die, they just fade away. Good-bye."

"I know Truman was right to get rid of him," Dad said, as he reached to turn off the switch. "But it's still sad, isn't it?"

"At least MacArthur knew how to bow out gracefully," Mom said.

Her words surprised me. In the nine years my parents had owned our grocery, my mother had been the fighter, doing what she could to keep the business on its feet. It was Mom who made sure bills were paid on time, Mom who tried to rein in Dad's careless spending, and Mom who prevented customers from piling on too much debt. I never expected her to applaud an exit line.

"What time should we close up?" Dad asked, changing the subject.

"No one's been in for hours. It's time."

Then, she reached across the counter to steer away Dad's hand that was hovering over a Baby Ruth candy bar. That was another thing Mom had tried to keep in check—Dad's overeating despite doctors' warnings about his diabetes. Was she tiring of that battle, too?

"Maybe Feldman will come in," Dad said. "I haven't seen her this week. We should stay open for her. She'll need bread and milk for the morning."

"Wake up, Irv," Mom said, moving a butt-filled ashtray to Dad's side of the counter. "She shops at the A&P, the same as Schwartz."

"So, a couple of *momsers* try and save a few bucks by going across Division. There's enough customers to keep us going," Dad said, lighting up a Camel. He took a drag from the cigarette, and his cough erupted a miniature volcano in the ashtray, spilling flakes over its lips onto the counter.

"Where, tell me where they are?" Mom said, as she used the edge of her hand to sweep the ashes back into their container. Wiping soot from her palm onto her apron, she continued: "The Levinsons just moved to Albany Park, near my sister Mollie. Your precious poolroom's gone, the Division Street we know is gone. Open your eyes."

At the mention of the poolroom, Dad's eyes clouded, and he continued taking deep drags of his cigarette. I recalled the sad conversation that followed the poolroom's demise. Mom and I were seated at the kitchen table at the back of our grocery store when Dad came in with the news. I was doing homework, Mom was reviewing bills, and my 15-year-old brother Ronnie was at his part-time job at Sammy's Red Hots across the street.

"Television," Dad had said. "Everyone's locked up in their apartments staring at black-and-white screens. It's ruined social life. It killed the poolroom."

"Look who's talking," Mom had said, looking up from her stack. "You're glued to the Cubs on WGN-TV and the Friday night fights."

Dad nodded his head and sank into a chair that creaked at his weight. "I know," he had said. "I take the blame, too. I'm just saying, I miss the old days."

I often felt the same way about television and its effect on friendships, for there were times when I chose *The Mary Hartline Show, Kukla, Fran, and Ollie;* or even Buffalo Bob Smith and *Howdy Doody* over games with my pals. It was hard to face, but my small world had faded since my parents first bought the store in 1942. One by one, my cousins and my friends had left for the north side, Skokie, or elsewhere. The sidewalk in front of our grocery store no longer served as our neighborhood playlot or community center. Television, suburban backyards, and supermarkets were draining our close-knit block of its friendliness, its familiarity.

The sound of the bell above the store's entry startled me, and I turned to see who was coming in. My parents' faces brightened, hoping, I suppose, for a paying customer, but instead we heard:

"Hi. In the neighborhood. Thought I'd stop by and pick up the check." It was the Bowman Dairy driver.

"Can you give us more time?" Mom asked, her eyes glancing down at the red inked-figures in the ledger book.

"Just a couple of days?" Dad said, dropping his cigarette on the floor and grinding it out with the tip of his shoe. His force made me wonder if it was the glowing butt he was trying to extinguish, or the defecting customers who owed us money but shopped elsewhere.

"Yeah, sure," the milkman said, keeping one hand on the open door. "But the boss is on my back, and I don't know how long he'll carry you."

Dad approached the visitor and clasped his crisp white cotton shoulder. "Thanks," he said, "you're a mensch. Just a few more days."

After the milkman left, Mom punched a key of her Burroughs register and the drawer exploded out towards her body. Like a lightweight avoiding a punch to the gut, Mom hopped back, then removed the paper bills and coins.

"We both could get jobs," she said, as she counted out the money.

Jobs, what's this about? What are they talking about? I asked myself. I kept still and listened for more clues.

"What about the kids?" Dad said, returning from the front door to his spot opposite my mother. "I thought we were building something for the kids."

"Ronnie doesn't even work in the store anymore," Mom said. "He makes more money at the hotdog stand. And half the time, he's up in Albany Park with his high school buddies. What does he care about a *farshtunken* [stinking] grocery store? And Elaine's got her head in the books. She's never going to work behind a counter. She'll go to college. She'll be a teacher, you'll see."

"I don't think I can do it. We've put so much into it," my father said, staring at the shelves lining the walls. His eyes gazed at the boxes of cereal, sacks of sugar, and cans of cut-up fruit. He looked wistful then, as if the merchandise were his long-gone poolroom cronies, not out-of-date stock.

"It'll be painless," Mom said gently, reaching across the counter to touch Dad's shoulder. Her tender voice and gesture caught my attention as much as MacArthur's speech had, for it was odd to hear Mom address Dad without irritation. I starred in disbelief as she took a Baby Ruth from its display carton and moved it towards Dad's fingers.

"We'll call in a broker, he'll figure it out," she said. "Then it'll be over, finished, and we can get on with our lives. Look, I doubt if we can even sell the place. Who's going to buy a *pisher* ma-and-pa store when there's a brand-new supermarket on every block. An auction may be the only way to go."

"Things could get better," Dad said, taking a bite of the candy bar and reviving like a flattened boxer coming to. Then, possibly emboldened by her gift, he reached across to caress Mom's arm, and said, "I'd miss you."

"We'll see each other at dinner, at breakfast. We'll tell each other what happened during the day, about our *meshuggana* bosses, our coworkers," she said.

"It won't be the same," Dad said, keeping his hand where it was happy to land.

"Nothing stays the same, but if you're totally against it, I can't force you."

"You always know what's best."

Mom stepped away to untie her apron, causing Dad's hand to flop to the counter. She slowly lifted the well-worn cloth over her head, careful not to muss her makeup or hairdo, then placed the folded apron upon the ledger book and returned both to their foxhole under the counter. Then, Dad rested his cigarette on the ashtray and removed his apron, too, tossing it on the floor behind the register.

"Elaine, let's go," Mom called to me. "We're closing up now." She walked to the front of the store and reached up to turn out the lights. When Mom's back was turned, Dad snatched two more Baby Ruths and two packs of Camels from full display cartons on the counter, then stuffed them in both pants pockets. As we walked to the door, Dad called out to her, "Wait for us." Reaching for my hand, he said to me, "Come, Princess, come with us." But Mom was already on the sidewalk, the dinging bell signaling her exit.

That evening in our apartment, I tried to ask my parents about the mysterious conversation downstairs, but they shushed me because Mayor Martin H. Kennelly was on the radio. He had just won a second term and was listing the new subways, superhighways, and street lighting that would "build us an even bigger and better city." The Chicago Housing Authority was speeding up slum clearance, and eight new low-rent housing projects were to be built.

Was Division Street a slum? I wondered. Some people called it a "Jewish ghetto" and that sounded like a slum to me. As I listened to the list of neighborhoods to be bulldozed, I was relieved to learn Division Street wasn't included. Although run-down, my old neighborhood would remain standing—a gateway for hopeful immigrants, as it once was for my very own parents.

After the mayor's broadcast, I tried again to learn our store's fate, but my parents dismissed me with, "Not now," or "We'll talk about it later." I knew that the following evening, April 20th, we'd be celebrating Passover at my *zadie*'s apartment, and that all of my mom's family would be there. If my parents were to discuss the store with a relative, I might be able to find out what was going on.

At age 12 going on 13, I had mixed feelings about the possibility of losing our business. On the one hand, like my dad, I'd miss seeing our family working side by side. But on the other hand, I wouldn't miss my parents' sparring, or seeing their disappointment as grocery profits sagged. What kind of jobs could they get in the outside world? I wondered. Could Dad's health handle such an upheaval? Would we move from Division Street, too? Would I still get to enroll at Roosevelt High, like my brother? These were four personal questions I hoped to get answered, sometime after the traditional Four Questions of the upcoming Seder service.

My grandfather, Harry Elkin, had married again after my *bubbie*'s death in 1949, and because my mother disliked his new wife, our visits to his apartment had faded. And although it was sad to be at a Pesach dinner with a new woman in *Bubbie*'s place, I looked forward to reuniting with my aunts, uncles, and cousins. As we walked up the stairs to *Zadie*'s second-floor flat, I noticed that the walls lining the stairwell were nearly the same as when my mother's brother Paul had stained them more than 10 years ago. With a kitchen sponge dipped into a bucket of turquoise paint, Uncle Paul had created textured swirls up and down the walls of the staircase.

I recalled being carried up these very same stairs by my mother's youngest brother, Hy, when I was about three years old, following a tonsillectomy. Uncle Hy had held me in his strong arms and promised "as much ice cream as you can eat." But still groggy from the procedure's ether and with a sore throat, I didn't reply. Instead, I wrapped one small arm around his neck and brushed the fingers of my dangling hand against the painted swirls every step of the way.

The sponged designs were chipped and fading this Passover of 1951, but visible enough to bring me back to that time of my childhood when my parents, brother, and I were living in my grandparents' apartment. It was in the early years of the war when rentals were hard to come by, and like many American families, we were doubling up. We took turns sleeping on a cot on an enclosed porch, on a living room sofa, or in an empty bedroom—depending upon the number of other relatives sharing the rooms. Despite the crowding, I never felt underprivileged back then, before we finally got our own place. In fact, I felt lucky to have all those loving relatives so close by.

The smells of Pesach foods, wafting down from the second-floor landing, interrupted my toddler flashback, and I followed my parents and brother up the stairs to the odors' source. Salty chicken soup with matzo balls, gefilte fish crowned with golden carrots, hills of chopped liver, roast brisket and chicken crackling with fat, and *tsmiss* cooked fruit awaited the Elkin clan (numbering nearly 30 that year) in Jewish-food heaven at the top of the stairs. When I entered the flat, I saw several long folding tables that stretched from the dining room into the living room, with card tables tucked on the farthest end for the kids.

As each family piled into the place, tossing jackets on the chenille spread of a spare bedroom, they were greeted with shouts of "Let's get started already, I'm starving." I noted where Aunt Etta and her husband, Maury Kaplan, were seated and rushed to a place that was on the kids' end, but nearest the two of them. If my folks were to reveal their plans to anyone, it would be to the Kaplans.

The folding tables were set in the traditional Pesach fashion: Each place setting held a Maxwell House Haggadah booklet that would provide the script for the Seder service. Plates of matzos and jars of pungent horseradish were within reach of each diner. Ceremonial plates that held the egg, shank bone, bitter herbs, parsley, haroset (apples, walnuts, wine, and cinnamon), and saltwater sat in the middle of the tables. Once settled and serious, the adults took turns reading passages from the Haggadah that retold the deliverance of the children of Israel from centuries of Egyptian bondage. In the course of the service, an aunt or uncle asked a question to determine a child's knowledge of the holiday. And one by one, the four questions were answered, haltingly, by younger cousins whose brows were furrowed in concentration, and who tracked the English translations with their tiny index fingers.

Pressured by the hungry crowd, the adult readers sped through their passages until the final chant, "Next year in Jerusalem." Then came the slapping of booklets and the joyous cries of, "Let's eat!"

My mother left her chair to join the other women who were bringing out the menu's first course. Like tightrope walkers, each returned slowly from the kitchen balancing a plate brimming with hot soup, cooked carrots, and a fat matzo ball. Dad was seated next to Uncle Maury, his mouth watering and his brown eyes fixed on the women's treacherous steps.

I could hear their topic, General MacArthur's speech. Confident I wasn't missing any news of the store, I turned to a conversation underway on my end:

"I read an article in *The Saturday Evening Post* that said by 1954 the Reds could drop 150 atom bombs on American cities," said my cousin Warren Silver. Although six months younger than I, my aunt Mollie's eldest son was a foot taller and that much smarter in his knowledge of world events. Dressed in a long-sleeved shirt with cuffs that stopped short of his wrists, and navy blue slacks, my lanky cousin looked like a young Jimmy Stewart.

"We had an atom bomb drill in school," my cousin Estherly said, as she pushed up the sleeves of her lace-trimmed blouse. "Some of us stayed at our desks and ducked our heads, while other kids crouched along the hallway. It was scary." As she spoke, I grew wistful. Estherly was now living on the South Side, worlds away it seemed, from our days together on Division Street. I smiled as I remembered our Saturday afternoon dancing lessons: Estherly, fair-skinned and tall in her ballerina costume; me, a brunette peanut in tap shoes. That was a fun time, I thought, hungry for another part of my childhood that had faded away.

"I heard about that atom bomb report," my brother Ronnie said, rolling up the sleeves of his argyle sweater. "It was called 'The Grim Truth About Civil Defense.'" Talk about grim, my big brother would turn 16 in less than a month,

A sunny day on Division Street with my parents, aunts, and cousins. From left to right: me, Dad, and Mom; Estherly, Aunt Etta, David; and Aunt Rose with Jay and Norman.

and the draft age was recently lowered to 18 years old. The possibility of A-bombs, and losing him to the Army in two years, frightened me more than the potential loss of the store.

I turned away from the discussion and tucked in on the food that had finally reached our end of the table. As I ate, savoring each spoonful, I peeked at my father. With one hand propping up his head, Dad looked like a palooka recovering from a blow.

"She's pushing me to sell," I heard him say to Uncle Maury as he jabbed a mound of gefilte fish. Both men wore short-sleeved white shirts, but Uncle Maury had on a tie, while my dad's shirt was unbuttoned at the collar. I couldn't see Dad's pants from where I was seated, but I knew that within a few more courses, he would unbuckle his belt, open the first button, and breathe a sigh of relief as his belly erupted beyond the waistband.

"Maybe it's for the best," Uncle Maury said, placing a hand on my dad's slumped shoulder. "The meat purveyor who comes to my butcher shop told me they're looking for salesmen, and if I knew anyone for the job, I should let him know."

"I used to be a salesman," Dad said, sitting up and squaring his shoulders like a champ. "Blue Star Auto Supply, remember?"

"Sure, you were the best. And you know meat. I could put a word in."

Perhaps it was the sustenance that appeared before my dad—one filled plate following each empty one—or maybe it was Uncle Maury's comforting words; but once again my father rallied. His brown eyes brightened, his greasy mouth turned up in a smile.

I caught up with my mother and Aunt Etta as they were paused at the stove waiting for the next course. The lineup of sisters and sisters-in-law reminded me of the brigades of volunteers I'd seen in movies of the Old West. In those films, men handed off buckets of water to douse a raging barn fire. Here, in *Zadie*'s steamy kitchen, it was the women who were hustling plates of chicken and brisket to hungry kinfolk in the next room.

I loitered at the bathroom door, pretending to wait for its occupant to exit. Folding my arms across the flat chest of my green lamb's wool sweater, and tapping the toe of my saddle shoe to feign impatience, I listened to my mother:

"I think I've got him convinced," she said to Aunt Etta.

"He's so crazy about you, he'll do anything you say," Aunt Etta said.

Although older than her sister, my mother was a half-foot shorter. Both slender women were attired for the holiday—in pretty rayon dresses with padded shoulders, nylon stockings, and round-toed high-heeled shoes.

"But it's for the best, isn't it?" Mom asked.

"Of course. How long can you keep losing money, getting deeper into debt?"

"I'd look for a job. The kids don't need me home anymore."

"You're so smart, anyone would hire you," Aunt Etta said, touching Mom's rouged cheek. "You'd be grabbed up in a minute."

My mother's eyes shone at Aunt Etta's prediction, and

I pictured my mom working in an office somewhere, admired for her brains as well as her beauty. "Great job, Min," would be daily compliments in her new 9-to-5 workplace. There might be a bit of flirting, too, from professional-type men who never stood behind a meat counter wearing a blood-smeared apron. From the look on Mom's face—so attractive and hopeful despite the kitchen heat that was fading her makeup and wilting her hair—I imagined she was fancying the very same scene.

Back at our flat that evening, my parents finally disclosed their decision to sell the store. The four of us were seated around the kitchen table, the smoke from Dad's cigarette hovering like a mushroom cloud over our heads. "You understand," Mom said to Ronnie and me, a plea in her voice. "The business is just not there, and it's not going to get any better."

Then Dad took over: "You won't have to worry about food on the table or a roof over your heads. We'll always provide for you."

"We're not worried," Ronnie said, rising from his place at the table. About to finish his freshman year at Roosevelt High, my brother was already a member of the most popular boys club at the school—the Jovens. His sunny personality and optimism reminded me of the movie star Mickey Rooney, eager to "put on a show" with Judy Garland. Ronnie squeezed Dad's shoulder and said, "Look, you came over from the old country, you didn't know the language, started from nothing. You became Americans, made a family, you opened your own business. You did great." I half expected to hear "Strike Up The Band," but there was only silence as my mother twisted her fingers to relieve years of aches, and my dad puffed steadily on his cigarette.

"You couldn't stop supermarkets, halt progress," Ronnie continued. "You have nothing to be ashamed of." Then, my mother and father turned to me, seeking, I'm sure, the same reassurance, the same plaudits.

"I understand, too," I assured them. "It's just like General MacArthur said in his farewell speech, it was the fulfillment of your hopes and dreams. But you two aren't going to fade away, are you? You're going to get back on your feet, better than ever!"

I'm not sure I believed my own pep talk that night, but I was certain it was what my parents needed to bolster them in the months ahead.

For several weeks following the verdict, our landlady Mrs. Newman, steered potential buyers through the grocery store. In foreign tongues, the men and women—who appeared to be of Greek, East Indian, Spanish, or other ethnicities—whispered to their partners as they inspected the deli case, ice cream cooler, walk-in freezer, and other fixtures. My parents and I stood on the sidelines and listened as our landlady added, "A little fixing up, that's all it needs." Her sloppy dress, torn handbag overflowing with papers, and sales spiel reminded me of our own first tour of the space. I recalled Mom's skepticism about the enterprise, Dad's eagerness, and my own excitement. I could even picture my two uncles and my grandfather all those

years ago—the butcher, fruit peddler, and fishmonger—
offering advice, encouragement, even cash.

Sadly, Mrs. Newman's tours produced no buyers, so
my parents decided on an auction of the store's fixtures as
the only solution to pay outstanding debts. (*Zadie* refused
a return of his original loan. "If I ever need the *gelt*, I'll
know where to find it," he said.)

On the day of the auction, my 42-year-old father and 38-
year-old mother, plus Ronnie and I, stood silently in the
rear of the store as the auctioneer's assistant went from
fixture to fixture, slapping a paper number on each surface. We watched as groups of people filed in—some were
prospective bidders, others curious neighbors, and a few
sympathetic relatives and friends.

Because we had done some dusting and tidying up
before the appointed hour, my parents were still wearing
their store aprons over their clothing. Ronnie and I had
dressed in dungarees and well-worn pullovers, just in case
we'd be called on to help buyers out with their winnings.

While waiting for the tagger to finish his task, I kept
an eye on my parents—anxious to monitor their moods.
Dad was smoking, staring at the cigarette ashes he had
flicked on the floor, perhaps wishing they were tea leaves
revealing his fortune.

As I watched my father, I pretended I was a child
again playing with paper doll cutouts. I mentally traded
Dad's getup with the new gabardine suit he'd be wearing
the following Monday. Uncle Maury had come through
for Dad and introduced him to the meat purveyor who

hired Dad on the spot. Ronnie and I had accompanied my parents to Mandel Brothers, where Dad purchased a sharp-looking double-breasted dark brown suit, two white shirts, and two wide patterned ties. In the department store's three-way mirror, Dad looked a winner, excited for a job that would pay a steady $80 a week.

As for my mother, she had perused the *Chicago Tribune* want ads, and as Aunt Etta had predicted, got hired in her first interview. "We'll teach you everything you need to know," a supervisor had told her about her new job as a switchboard operator for American Linen Supply Company. When Mom repeated his words to us on the day she was hired, and announced her own salary of $65 a week, she looked triumphant—like Vivien Leigh accepting the Academy Award for *A Streetcar Named Desire*. Mom was to start work the very same Monday as Dad, and I could visualize her dressed in the sky-blue jersey shirtwaist she had already selected for her first day.

As for me, I was content my life after the store would remain pretty much the same—no costume changes, save for pale pink lipstick on special occasions. There'd be no parent to welcome me home at 3:15; but at age 13, I welcomed the independence. Ronnie was okay with our parents' outside employment, as his world had already crossed the borders of our old neighborhood.

The auctioneer's gavel pounded us alert, and I turned my attention to the small crowd that had gathered. Aunt Etta, who had promised my mom she would be at her side this day, moved in close to put her arm around her sister's waist. Uncle Maury stood next to Dad—his arms crossed in front of him, just like my father's—their shields against any emotional blows.

My mother's friend, Rose Levinson, was there, too, kissing Mom's cheek in greeting. But when Mrs. Schwartz—whose debts led the list in Mom's ledger—attempted a similar gesture, Mom turned her face away. My dad, who had witnessed Mrs. Schwartz's approach, muttered under his breath—but loud enough for me to hear, "Bitch."

"What am I bid for the display case?" the auctioneer called out. All eyes turned to his accomplice, who was demonstrating the sliding glass doors that once opened onto fat tubes of salami, slabs of marbled steak, and pyramids of cut-up chicken, but now revealed barren shelves.

As the bidders called out dollar amounts—first for the deli case, then the Burroughs cash register, the salami slicer, the meat scale, and every other piece of equipment and crate of merchandise in the place—the auctioneer declared, "Going, going, gone!"

When it was all over, when new owners had claimed everything in the store, my family walked slowly around the space, touching the empty shelves for one last time.

We each carried out something. I was cradling my cigar box register that I had rescued from my sundries section, and Ronnie held the black-and-white photo he had lifted from its hook on my wall. Taken eight years earlier when Irv's Finer Foods had just opened, the photo showed the four of us, plus Dad's sweet sister, Mary, as we posed out front. As I gazed at the picture in my brother's young hands, I smiled at how it had captured us then—so eager to grab our share of the American dream.

Mom clasped the ledger book and Dad held a hand-lettered sign he had made earlier. As we neared the front door, my mother used two fingers to drop the ledger book into an overflowing wastebasket, and followed it with her store apron. Dad Scotch-taped the sign he was carrying to the plate glass window. "Store closed," it read. Then, after three of us had filed out, Dad untied his apron, too, and stuffed it in the trash. Finally, my father switched off the light and slowly shut the door, leaving Irv's Finer Foods, of 2505 W. Division Street, in Chicago's Humboldt Park neighborhood, behind us.

Epilogue

Seven years after my father closed the door on Irv's Finer Foods, I was in a college classroom with my head bent over a sociology textbook when a messenger entered the room and whispered something into the professor's ear. I looked up with the rest of the students, and my heart froze as the professor waved a hand to call me up to his desk. "There's a phone call for you in the office," he whispered.

It was January 9, 1958, and I was a sophomore at Roosevelt University in downtown Chicago majoring in education. As I raced down the marble steps of the school's grand staircase, I prayed aloud, "Not Daddy, please not Daddy."

I had carried this worry with me throughout my childhood, and after we closed the store and moved from Division Street in 1951. In the years since the auction, we had been living in a beautiful six-room apartment on the city's north side. Dad was a star salesman for the meat company, and Mom was excelling in her job as a switchboard operator. Separated from each other during the day, and relieved of the store's aggravations, my parents were a happier couple now, their bickering diminished.

My brother Ronnie had enlisted in the Army at 19, and while attending a Friday night service for Jewish GIs stationed in Fort Riley, Kansas, met the woman he eventually married. After a tour of duty in Hawaii, Ronnie moved to Kansas City to work for his father-in-law in his auto supply business. This was ironic, as my dad's first job in Chicago was as a salesman for Blue Star Auto Supply.

As for me, I spent four unremarkable years at Roosevelt High School with my best friend, Ruth; and after graduation, we both enrolled at Roosevelt University. A

*Nineteen-year-old Private
Ronnie Shapiro in 1954.*

Me (seated) and my best friend from Lafayette Grammar School, Roosevelt High School, Roosevelt University, and still today, Ruth Ross Gilbert.

scholarship and part-time job took care of my tuition, as my parents couldn't afford the cost of this private university. Although I had a few crushes and boyfriends, I was unattached at 20. Because most of my girlfriends were wearing diamond rings by now, I was hopeful I'd find a fiancé before college graduation in two years.

Panting from my sprint down the stairs, I grabbed the phone in the university's main office and managed a breathless "Hello."

"Your dad's had a heart attack." It was my uncle Hy, my mother's youngest brother, calling from the hospital. "Get here as soon as you can." I jumped into a cab that was parked on Michigan Avenue right outside the school's entrance, and directed the driver to Alexian Brothers on the far north side.

As I sat in the cab's back seat, my winter coat wrapped tightly around my shivering body, I continued to pray that my father would survive. As a child, I knew his health was precarious and I was often angry that he didn't take better care of himself. Do it for me, Daddy, I would think, stay alive for me. But when nagged to skip extra helpings, he'd say, "If I can't eat, I don't want to live." That was his decision, and I would just have to accept it. But any anger or bitterness I had felt at his choice faded during the taxi ride. All I wanted now was to find my father alive.

When I entered the hospital room, my mother was sobbing, and I could see that my uncle Hy had spared me the news that the heart attack was fatal. "Say good-bye to Daddy," my mother said to me, sagging in my aunt Etta's arms. Uncle Hy put his arm around my waist and walked with me to the bed. I kissed my 48-year-old father's cool forehead and said, "I love you." I had missed his final words, but knew what they would have been had I stood at his bedside. "I love you, too, Princess," he would have said. I was sure of it.

The Elkin boys all grown up: Hy, Nate, Carl, and Paul.

Acknowledgments

I would like to thank the following people:

My husband, Tom Madison, for his support and his eagerness to read every draft; Kay Marie Porterfield for her sharp editorial eye and belief in me; my daughter Jill for reading early drafts and guiding my publishing; my daughter Faith for her constant encouragement; and Ruth Ross Gilbert for our decades-long friendship and for sharing her experiences.

My brother, Ron Shapiro, a major character in this Division Street story; Renee Elkin, my cousin and photo editor; my aunt Etta Kaplan, and cousins Estherly Kaplan Reifman and Warren Silver for their memories; Gerald Shapiro for his professional eye; and Neil Shapiro for our cherished relationship. And first-reader friends Karen Carpino and Isolde Ralis for their encouraging reviews.

Other relatives, friends, and neighbors who have encouraged my writing: Harry Soloway, Judy Pearl (in memoriam), Hedy Ratner, Phil Rozen, Marshall Rosenthal, and

Susie Miller. Also, Dink Adams, Nelson Ameer, Carole Bellows, Norma Berlin, Kiyoki Binosi, Liz Copeland, Pat Dodson, Maureen Gorman, Sandra Levitan, Ruth Lieberman, Marshall Lobin, Patty Novik, Inna Pogosyan, Ilene Shapiro, Norma Shapiro, Penny and Tim Shultz, Bob Singer, Hal "Tiger" Temkin, and Holly and John Van Essen.

Writers and PR gurus who have been in my corner: Harlyn Aizley, Lucia Annunzio, Mary Grigar, Sandy House, Mort Kaplan, Syd Lieberman, Danny Miller, Chris Ruys, and Michele Snyder. Former bosses, clients, and mentors who enhanced my career: Mayor Jane M. Byrne, Doris Payne Camp, Steve Crews, Rick Jasculca, Marilyn Katz, Ruth R. Love, Marilyn Panichi, Larry Schaffel, and Jim Terman.

Writing group teachers and members who listened, aided, and inspired my writing: S. L. Wisenberg; Richard Hollinger and the St. Charles Writing Group, especially Mike Balcom-Vetillo, Sue Glavan, Kitty Jarman, Susan Kraykowski, Bonnie Harn Petkus, and Bruce Steinberg; and Margaret Schmidt and the Newberry Library Life Stories Workshop.

Fellow Dog Parkers who have tolerated my 6:00 a.m. updates: Lucy Aiello, Loretta Aylward, Russ Bliss, Ivan and Sara Clatanoff, Paula Giroux, Rob Miller, Mary Rebello, Lisa Reed, Molly Reed, Susan Shaw, Soroya Tonos, Paul Tyler, and Candace Wayne.

And Tommy's supportive crew: Vicky and Randy Bates, Brenda Berman, Barry Bruner, Ann and Bill Newman, and Jill and Ron Rohde.

Finally, and most importantly, to my publishing team at Syren Book Company: Mary Byers, Wendy Holdman, Kyle Hunter, Ann Sudmeier, and Maria Manske.

A deep bow of gratitude to all.

Elaine Soloway is a public relations consultant and free-lance writer whose essays have appeared in the *New York Times Money & Business, Chicago Tribune WomanNews, ActiveTimes Magazine, Today's Chicago Woman, Chicago Jewish News*; and Web Sites: 2Young2Retire.com, jewishmag.com, skirtmag.com, freshyarn.com, and chijewishnews.com. In her career, Elaine served as a press aide to Chicago mayor Jane Byrne and school superintendent Ruth Love. She lives in Chicago with her husband, Tom, and golden retriever, Buddy, and has two daughters and two grandchildren. Both daughters are in the entertainment industry: Faith is a musician and producer of rock operas who also works in a violence prevention program with the Boston public schools. Jill lives in Los Angeles and was a writer on the HBO series *Six Feet Under* and is the author of *Tiny Ladies in Shiny Pants* (Free Press).

To order additional copies of *The Division Street Princess*

Web: www.itascabooks.com

Phone: 1-800-901-3480

Fax: Copy and fill out the form below with credit card information. Fax to 763-398-0198.

Mail: Copy and fill out the form below. Mail with check or credit card information to:

Syren Book Company
5120 Cedar Lake Road
Minneapolis, MN 55416

Order Form

Copies	Title / Author	Price	Totals
	***The Division Street Princess / * Elaine Soloway**	$15.95	$
		Subtotal	$
		7% sales tax (MN only)	$
		Shipping and handling, first copy	$ 4.00
		Shipping and handling, ___ add'l copies @$1.00 ea.	$
		TOTAL TO REMIT	$

Payment Information:

__ Check Enclosed   __ Visa/MasterCard
Card number: Expiration date:
Name on card:
Billing address:
City: State: Zip:
Signature: Date:

Shipping Information:

__ Same as billing address   __ Other (enter below)
Name:
Address:
City: State: Zip: